Patrik Schumacher

Digital Hadid
Landscapes in Motion

Birkhäuser – Publishers for Architecture
Basel • Boston • Berlin

A CIP catalogue record for this book is available from the Library of Congress, Washington D.C., USA.

Deutsche Bibliothek Cataloging-in-Publication Data

Bibliographic information published by Die Deutsche Bibliothek
Die Deutsche Bibliothek lists this publication in the Deutsche Nationalbibliografie; detailed bibliographic data is available on the Internet at <http://dnb.ddb.de>.

This work is subject to copyright. All rights are reserved, whether the whole or part of the material is concerned, specifically the rights of translation, reprinting, re-use of illustrations, recitation, broadcasting, reproduction on microfilms or in other ways, and storage in data banks. For any kind of use permission of the copyright owner must be obtained.

Original edition:
Hadid Digitale (Universale di Architettura, collana fondata da Bruno Zevi; La Rivoluzione Informatica, sezione diretta da Antonino Saggio).
© 2004 Testo & Immagine, Turin

© 2004 Birkhäuser – Publishers for Architecture, P.O. Box 133, CH-4010 Basel, Switzerland.
Part of Springer Science+Business Media Publishing Group.
Printed on acid-free paper produced from chlorine-free pulp. TCF ∞
Printed in Italy
ISBN 3-7643-0172-4

9 8 7 6 5 4 3 2 1   http://www.birkhauser.ch

Contents

Introduction	4
I. The Prehistory of the New Digitally Based Architecture	8
The Quest for New Design Media	8
Zaha Hadid in Her Own Words	10
Graphic Space	15
Post-modernism, Deconstructivism, Folding	21
Mechanisms of Invention	26
II. Current Work. Towards a New Digitally Based Architectural Language	30
Organic Interarticulation	30
Center for Contemporary Arts, Rome	33
Art Center, Graz	38
Quebec National Library, Montreal	40
One North Masterplan, Singapore	44
BMW Plant - Central Building, Leipzig	47
Ice-storm, Lounging Environment	52
Z-scape, Lounging Furniture	56
BBC Music Centre and Office, London	59
Fine Arts Center, University of Connecticut	66
Fast Train Station, Florence	69
Fast Train Station, Naples	74
The Temporary Guggenheim, Tokyo	80
Guggenheim Museum, Taichung	83
Further Reading	89
Project Credits	90

Introduction

Digital Hadid will explore the contribution of Zaha Hadid and of Zaha Hadid Architects to the development of the new architectural language and paradigm that is fast becoming hegemonic within avant-garde architecture today.

There is an unmistakable new style manifest within avant-garde architecture today. Its most striking characteristic is its complex and dynamic curve-linearity. Beyond this obvious surface feature, one can identify a series of new concepts and methods that are so different from the repertoire of both traditional and modern architecture that one might speak of the emergence of a new paradigm for architecture. It seems difficult to give a unified name to this new paradigm that succinctly captures the essence of the current trend. One difficulty lies in the question whether such a defining term should refer to the formal features, the guiding concepts or the methods/techniques that characterize this new paradigm. Contenders are Blob-architecture, Folding, Deformation, Parametric Architecture, Digital Architecture.

This new language (or style) of architecture seems to be based upon the adoption of a new generation of 3D modeling tools. Indeed, a lot of commentators tend to construe a direct causal link from this new paradigm back to the IT revolution that has transformed the discipline in the last 10 years.

Indeed, the choice of a representational/design medium has a huge impact on the character of the design results. The medium is never neutral and external to the work. It constitutes and limits the design issues treated and the universe of possibilities for effective design speculation. Design thinking is bound to the representational medium and its scope can be expanded by the expansion offered by the new digital design tools. The reflection upon "design worlds" (Mitchell 1990), and their embeddedness in the "discursive formations" (Foucault 1972) of the discipline, are a necessary component of taking a progressive stance towards the possibilities of design research.

However, I shall argue and demonstrate that such a simple reduction of the new type of work to the availability of computing in architecture would be a fallacy. While it is undeniably true that the arrival of the new tools (3ds max a.o.) had a huge impact, and that these tools have been able to monopolize the production of contemporary work – without these tools nothing goes – I will argue that the adoption of animation tools was not at all inevitable, but rather had to be prepared by certain conceptual and methodological advances that preceded the arrival of these tools. To uncover and explicate this pre-digital pedigree of the current digital architecture will be the task of the first part of the book. In this prehistory one can locate Zaha Hadid's most original and path-breaking contributions to the development of contemporary architecture. In this era – the 1980s – Hadid was one of the key protagonists in a field of radical conceptual and formal architectural research, and her pre-eminent reputation was established on the basis of pictorial research without the completion of a single building during this first decade of her career. During this period, the computer was absent from Hadid's design studio. However, the innovation of certain analog design media deployed was crucial in the formation of her work.

The second part of the book will focus on the development of the work since the introduction of the computer in 1990. Here I will introduce a series of key projects and key concepts that have been important with respect to the development of the current flourishing of "digital architecture" both within and beyond Hadid's practice. This period is also the period in which Hadid's architecture made the transition from concept to material realization without compromising its innovative thrust. The involvement of the 3D modeling tools in this process of realization will be explained. Finally, I will present and discuss the most recent work of Zaha Hadid Architects, which is marked by the fact that a new level of structural complexity, tectonic fluidity and plastic articulation has been mastered with precision and confidence.

While the book presents two parts representing two phases in the development of Hadid's œuvre – pre-digital and (post)digital – I think the work has a strong overall continuity. The computer was introduced in the late eighties, early nineties, when we started with simple forms of 3D modeling with Model-shop and later FormZ. That was a process parallel to hand drafting and painting. They were quick three-dimensional sketches. The computer was used because it was helpful for what was already established as an architectural language. The computer programs that work with splines and smoothly deformable meshes were introduced much later, in the second half of the nineties. The 2D computer-drafting, for the plans and sections, started in the mid-nineties. That was a big shift, because it meant not just working in layers, which you can also do on transparent paper, but it meant that we could work on all plans simultaneously. The latest shift is the introduction of 3D modeling and complex curve-linearity. That made more complex compositions possible. But the desire for complex form was always building upon the formal and conceptual innovations achieved previously. The tools came in as soon as they were available, keenly taken up to support the ambitious design maneuvers already under way. It was a dialectic amplification, in which the new work spurned the search for new tools and the introduction of new tools facilitated the work further, pushing the most ambitious tendencies to new extremes. This process was an evolution of many smaller steps, not of a few singular breaks.

I. The Prehistory of the New Digitally Based Architecture

The Quest for New Design Media

One of the most significant and momentous features of the architectural avant-garde of the last 20 years is the proliferation of representational media and design processes.
In the early eighties, Zaha Hadid burst onto the architectural scene with a series of spectacular designs embodied by even more spectacular drawings and paintings. The idiosyncrasies of these drawings made it difficult to read them as straightforward architectural descriptions.
This initial openness of interpretation might have led some commentators to suspect "mere graphics" here.
There is an obvious parallel with the skepticism which confronted the early, abstract experiments in computer surface modeling in the mid-nineties.
However, these unusual modes of representation played a fundamental role in the development of a series of highly original and influential expansions of the formal and conceptual repertoire of architecture. Modes of representation in architecture are at the same time modes of generation. The creative process to a large extent resides in these modes and means. The creativity and information processing capacity of the "imagination" or "inner eye" is rather limited and is itself dependent upon being trained and developed in conjunction with the development of the media. That is why *Digital Hadid* is part of a significant series of investigations.

Computer technology, i.e. the new digital design tools, have had an important and increasing influence on the work of Zaha Hadid Architects over the last 10 years. This concerns primarily the handling of increasingly complex geometries within the designs. However, the desire for such tools to be imported from the animation industry originated in the fact that the tendency towards complexity and fluidity was already manifest in the work before those tools were available. Hadid's early elaborate techniques of projective distortion – deployed as a cohering device to elements as transparent to reveal the depth of the composition. This transparent superposition of the elements of a drawing anticipates the literal spatial interpenetration of geometric figures in order to create more complex organizations.

A third characteristic of Hadid's early work that anticipates a pervasive preoccupation of the recent avant-garde is the idea of manipulating the ground plane by means of cutting and warping (Tomigaya, Al Whada, Düsseldorf). This elaboration of the ground as manipulated/moulded surface anticipates the current use of digital surface modelers and the attendant idea of architectural articulation by means of surface foldings, implying the concept of the building as a single continuous surface.

Zaha Hadid in Her Own Words

Here is what Zaha Hadid had to say about the role of design media in general and digital media in particular in an interview with the Chairman of the Architectural Association School of Architecture Mohsen Mostafavi (El Croquis 103):

MM: You touched on the question of mechanisms or means of representation. How do you think your approach has changed in the last 5 or 10 years? What is the tension between your own drawings/conceptualizations and the way in which in your own office computers are playing such a central role ?

ZH: I still think that even in our later projects, where the computer was already involved, like for instance the IIT project, the 2-dimensional plan drawings are still seminal. I still think the plan is critical. The computer shows what you might see from various selected viewpoints. But I think this doesn't give you enough transparency; it's much too opaque. Also, I think it is much nicer on the screen than when it is printed onto paper, because the screen gives you luminosity and the paper does not, unless you do it through a painting. Further, I think if you compare computer renderings with rendering by hand, I must say that you can improvise much more with hand drawing and painting. As you go along, there is another layer of operation while you're working on the drawing which is somehow missing in the computer rendering. Some people still gather a multitude of elements into one geometric force field – were already setting the precedence of the current computer-based techniques of deformation and the modeling of fields by means of pseudo-gravitational forces.

Hadid used axonometric and perspective projection in a new way to dynamize the implied space. Initially, such projections were deployed according to their proper function as means of representation. However, it soon became apparent that there was a "self-serving" fascination with the extreme distortion of spaces and objects that emerged from the ruthless application of perspective construction – not unlike the anamorphic projections one can find in certain 17th-century paintings. Hadid built up pictorial spaces within which multiple perspective constructions were fused into a seamless, dynamic texture. One way to understand these images is as an attempt to emulate the experience of moving through an architectural composition revealing a succession of rather different points of view. Another, more radical way of reading these canvasses is to abstract from the implied views and to read the swarms of distorted forms as a peculiar architectural world in its own right with its own characteristic forms, compositional laws and spatial effects. One of the striking features of these large canvasses is their strong sense of coherence despite the richness and diversity of forms contained within them. There is never the order of monotonous repetition, but the field continuously changes its grain of articulation. Gradient transitions mediate large, quiet areas with very dense and intense zones. Usually these compositions are poly-central and multi-directional. All these features are the result of the use of multiple, interpenetrating perspective projections. Often the dynamic intensity of the overall field is increased by using curved instead of straight projection lines. The projective geometry lets an arbitrarily large and divers set of elements to be brought under its cohering law of diminution and distortion. The resultant graphic space greatly anticipates the later (and still very much current) concepts of *field* and *swarm*. The effect achieved is very much like the effects currently pursued with curve-linear mesh-deformations and digitally simulated "gravitational fields" that grip, align, orient and thus cohere a set of elements or particles within the digital model.

A second, prevalent feature of Hadid's large paintings is the technique of layering and the concomitant technique of rendering have this raw talent. Some people can do drawings and plans (by hand or by computer). They can manipulate them so much. Somebody like Patrik can do plans like nobody else. Some people have an incredible way of dealing with 3-dimensional modelling in the computer; but they don't have the same value. You can achieve certain things through technology. But you can't abstract in the same way. When drawing a perspective by hand, you can decide that you want to show and edit out some other things. It's not about wire-framing. Rather, you can decide to focus on the thing you want study at the same time as you're doing the drawing. It focuses you more on certain critical issues. However, because I'm sitting there with 15 or 20 computer screens in front of me and I can see them all at the same time, it gives me yet another repertoire. You can see at the same time the section, the plan and several moving 3D views, and in your mind you can see them in yet a different way. So I'm not sure if it weakens or strengthens your view. I just think it's a different way. And we still do physical models all the time, and I still do the sketches.

MM: With your drawings you were often dealing with a certain notion of distortion, which allowed certain conventions to be looked at again.

ZH: Yes, but what is interesting is that these ideas, at the time we did these drawings, allowed us to see a project from every possible and impossible perspective. Maybe you can do that now with the kind of animated fly-over. You can. But the nice thing about the elaborate drawing is that, because they take such a long time to construct, they give you the time to add many layers. With physical models, it is the peculiar nature of the material which affords design opportunities. Because I am always doing the contouring of the site in plexi, we began to see a similarity between liquid space and rock. Such "discoveries" can be productive. By the sheer use of the model, almost by total accident, you begin to look at things in different ways. So I'm saying that the presentation began to inform the work and it gives you ideas. In the case of the Tomigaya project in Tokyo, we did these very difficult drawings where we saw everything simultaneously in 3D. This coincided at the time with the appearance of the plexi model, about 15 years ago. What does it mean to see in a transparent

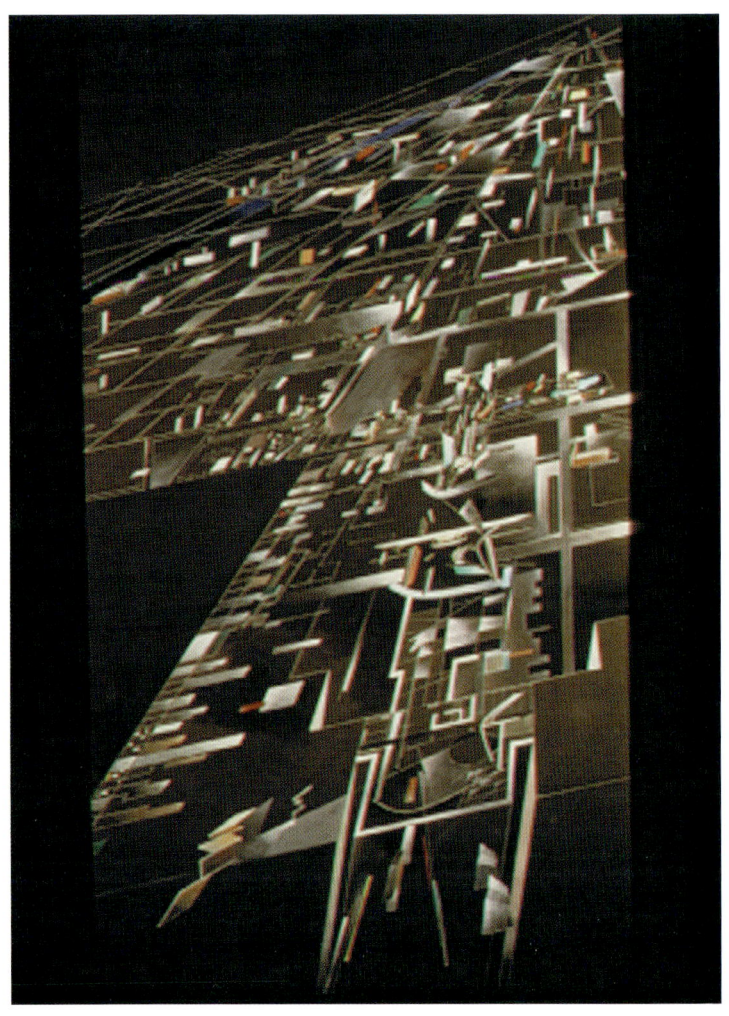

Rooftops, *London, 1985.*

way through a building? One of the implications for us was the realization that we do not have to have the vertical circulation operate like an extrusion or vertical core, but rather allow the vertical path to shift from one level to the next. This was discovered

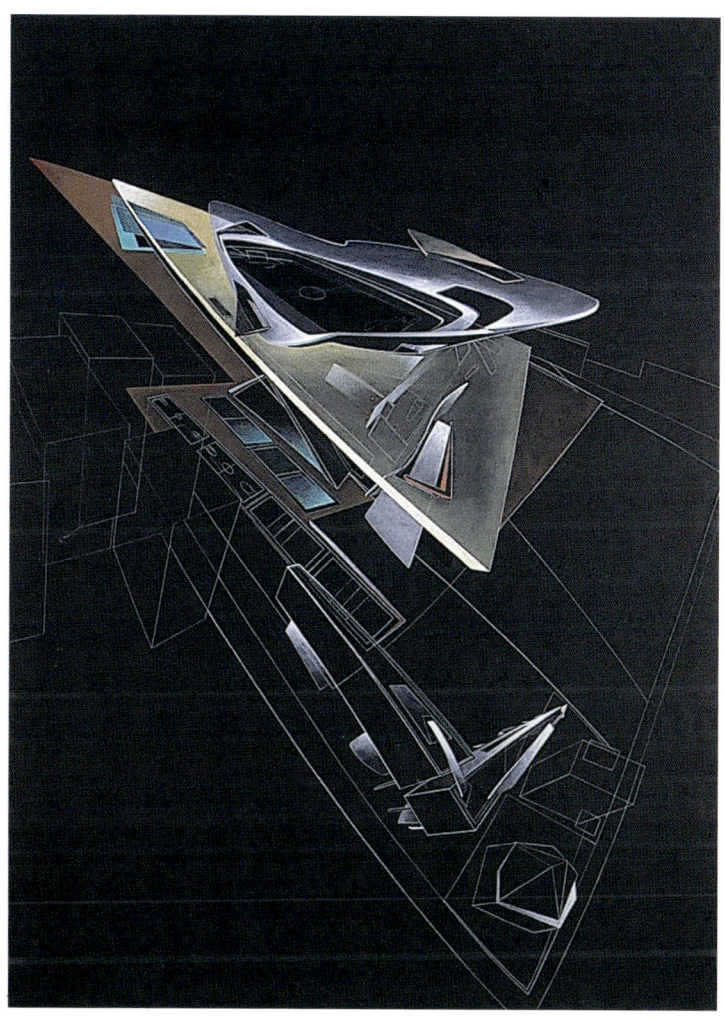

Al Whada Stadium, Abu Dhabi, 1988.

because we had the different plans overlaid with each other, to construct a way to connect the levels in a new way.
I think that, in a way, one can say that these very elaborate, complicated drawings – without saying that they are definitely finished

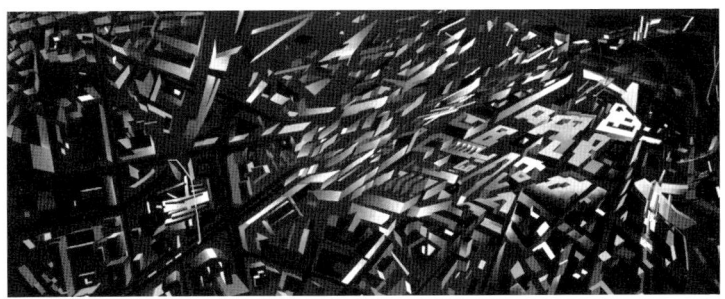

Victoria City Areal Development, Berlin, 1988.

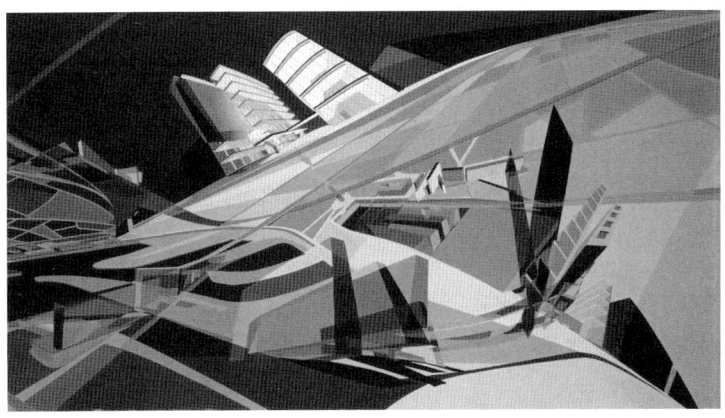

Art and Media Center, Düsseldorf, 1989-1993.

– did their job at the time. At the time, I could not present the work in a normative way. The work could not be done just through a simple set of plans and sections. There was an element of shock, really, which was to shock or challenge normal conventions. But it's not enough to just, say, do anything formally different. I think that 20 years ago, when my formal repertoire had developed over a number of years, in every project, the idea of the project was first challenged, and then it was worked on formally. We never set out explicitly with the intention of formal discovery, through a drawing with the prediction that we would discover something. All these drawings which were quite elaborate needed a scenario. These drawings were developed over a considerable length of time. Therefore, I would say, the formal repertoire that emerged was not completely accidental, perhaps a bit of accident at the beginning, prior to the development of the project. But then those accidental discoveries were worked out through very precise drawings.

Graphic Space

The predicament to start (and ultimately stay) with drawings, i.e. with objects lacking the third dimension, has been architecture's predicament ever since its inception as a discipline distinguished from construction. As Robin Evans pointed out so bluntly: architects do not build, they draw.
Therefore, the translation from drawing to building is always problematic – at least under conditions of innovation.
Architecture as a design discipline that is distinguished from the physical act of building constitutes itself on the basis of drawing. The discipline of architecture emerges and separates from the craft of construction through the differentiation of the drawing as a tool and domain of expertise outside (and in advance) of the material process of construction.
The first effect of drawing (in ancient Greek architecture) seems to be an increased capacity of standardization, precision and regularized reproduction on a fairly high level of complexity and across a rather wide territory. Roman architecture benefits from this but also shows a move towards the exploitation of the capacity of invention that the medium of drawing affords. Without drawing, the typological proliferation of Roman architecture is inconceivable. Since the Renaissance (via Mannerism and Baroque), this speculative moment of drawing has been gathering momentum. But only 1920s Modernism really discovers the full power and potential of drawing as a highly economic trial-error mechanism and an effortless plane of invention – in fact inspired by the compositional liberation achieved by abstract art in the first decade of the 20th century. Drawing accelerates the evolution of architecture. In this respect, modern architecture depends upon the revolution within the visual arts that finally shook off the burden of representation. Modern architecture was

able to build upon the legacy of modern abstract art as the conquest of a previously unimaginable realm of constructive freedom. Hitherto art was understood as mimesis and the reiteration of given subjects, i.e. re-presentation rather than creation. Architecture was the re-presentation of a fixed set of minutely determined typologies and complete tectonic systems. Against this backdrop, abstraction meant the possibility and challenge of free creation. The canvas became the field of an original construction. A monumental breakthrough with enormous consequences for the whole of modern civilization. Through figures such as Malevich and vanguard groups such as the De Stijl movement, this exhilarating historical moment was captured and exploited for the world of experimental architecture.

My thesis here is that the withdrawal into the two-dimensional surface, i.e. the refusal to interpret everything immediately as a spatial representation, is a condition for the full exploitation of the medium of drawing as a medium of invention. Only on this basis, as explicitly graphic maneuvers, do the design maneuvers gain enough fluidity and freedom to play. They have to be set loose, shake off the burden, to always already mean something determinate. Obviously, this stage of play and proliferation has to be followed by a tenacious work of selection and interpretation. At some stage, architectural work leads to building. But not in every "project". Some architectural projects remain "paper projects" which are "translated" later, by other projects. The discipline of architecture has learned to allow for this. Major contributions to the history of architecture have been made on this basis. Today, we see architectural experiments and manifestos proliferating within the virtual space afforded by the computer. Although the working interface (computer screen) as well as the various output media (printing, video-projection) remain strictly two-dimensional, the virtual three-dimensionality afforded by 3D modeling software offers a new way of working that combines the intuitive possibilities of physical model-making with the precision and immateriality of drawing. Further, as will be discussed in more depth below, certain 3D modeling and animation tools introduce whole new series of "primitives" and manipulative operations which are highly suggestive with respect to new architectural morphologies and the conceptual build-up of an architectural composition. However, these new compositional techniques still share some of

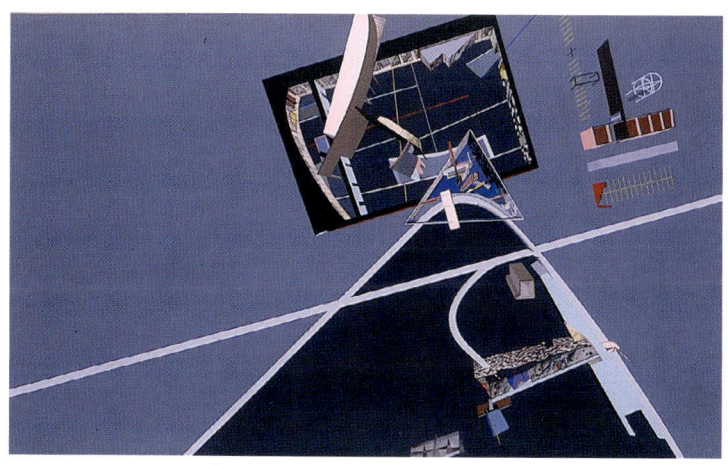

Irish Prime Minister's residence, Dublin, 1979-1980.

the productive under-determination of the experimental drawing. 3D modeling can be equally abstract and ambiguous with respect to the final translation into physical constructs.

One of Hadid's most audacious moves was to translate the dynamism and fluidity of her calligraphic hand directly into equally fluid tectonic systems. Another incredible move was the move from isometric and perspective projection to literal distortions of space and from the exploded axonometry to the literal explosion of space into fragments, from the superimposition of various fisheye perspectives to the literal bending and meltdown of space etc. All these moves initially appear rampantly illogical, akin to the operations of the surrealists.
The level of experimentation reached a point where the distinction between form and content within these drawings and paintings was no longer fixed. The question, which features of the graphic manipulation pertain to the mode of representation rather than to the object of representation, was left unanswered. Was the architecture itself twisting, bending, fragmenting and interpenetrating or were these features just aspects of the multi-viewpoint fisheye perspectives? The answer is that over an

extended process and a long chain of projects, the graphic features slowly transfigured into realizable spatial features. The initial openness in this respect might have led some commentators to suspect "mere graphics" here. Within Zaha Hadid's studio, this uncertainty was productively engaged through a slow process of interpretation via further drawings, projects and finally buildings.

These strange moves which seemed so alien and "crazy" – once taken seriously within the context of developing an architectural project – turn out to be powerful compositional options when faced with the task of articulating complex programs. The dynamic streams of movements within a complex structure can now be made legible as the most fluid regions within the structure; overall trapezoidal distortions offer one more way to respond to non-orthogonal sites; perspective distortions allow the orientation of elements to various functional focal points etc. What once was an outrageous violation of logic has become part of a strategically deployed repertoire of nuanced spatial organization and articulation.
Painterly techniques like color modulations, gradients of dark to light or pointillist techniques of dissolving objects into their background assume significance in terms of the articulation of new design concepts like morphing or new spatial concepts like smooth thresholds, "field-space" and the "space of becoming"(Eisenman). These concepts came to full fruition only with the latest digital 3D modeling and animation software. Jeff Kipnis deserves recognition here as someone who has theorized such possibilities of "graphic space". But it was Zaha Hadid who went first and furthest in exploring this way of innovating architecture – without, as well as with, the support of advanced software.

Zaha Hadid has been a persistent radical in the field of architectural experimentation for the last 20 years. The importance of her contribution to the culture of architecture lies primarily in a series of momentous expansions – as influential as they are radical – in the repertoire of spatial articulation available to architects today. These conquests for the design resources of the discipline include representational devices, graphic manipulations, compositional maneuvres, spatial concepts, typological inventions and (beyond the supposed remit of the discipline proper) the suggestion of new modes or patterns of inhabitation. This list of contributions describes a causal chain that significantly moves from the superficial to the substantial and thus reverses the order of ends vs. means assumed in normative models of rationality. The project starts as a shot into the dark, spreading its trajectories and assuming its target in midcourse. The point of departure is the assumption of new representational media (x-ray layering, multi-perspective projection) which allow for certain graphic operations (multiple, over-determining distortions) which then are made operative as compositional transformations (fragmentation and deformation). These techniques lead to a new concept of space (magnetic field space, particle space, continuously distorted space) which suggests a new orientation, navigation and inhabitation of space. The inhabitant of such spaces no longer orients by means of prominent figures, axis, edges and clearly bounded realms. Instead, the distribution of densities, directional bias, scalar grains and gradient vectors of transformation constitute the new ontology defining what it means to be somewhere. These innovations have been (and continue to be) produced within an international collective/competitive milieu of experimenters. The totality of discoveries emerging within this milieu is immediately appropriated – and rightly so – by each and every contributor.

This assessment of Hadid's oeuvre in terms of the expansion of architectural methods and formal resources is independent of the success and merit of the various built and unbuilt projects with respect to the particular tasks they are addressed to solve. Rather than fulfilling only their immediate purpose as a state of the art delivery of a particular use-value – e.g. a fire station or an exhibition venue – the significance and ambition of these projects is that they might be seen as manifestos of a new type of space. As such, their defining context is the historical progression of such manifestos rather than their concrete spatial and institutional location. The defining ancestry of the Vitra Fire Station or the Millennium Mind Zone, for example, includes the legacy of modern architecture and abstract art as the conquest of a previously unimaginable realm of constructive freedom. A key example for such a manifesto building is Rietveld's Schroeder House. The value and justification of this building does not only depend on the particular suitability to the Schroeder's family interests. It operates as an inspiring manifesto for new compositional possibilities, which much later are further extended in the Vitra Fire Station – Hadid's first built manifesto to be understood within Zaha Hadid's oeuvre at large. Both these manifesto buildings radically violate the typological and tectonic norms of their time and dare to suggest compositional moves hitherto unknown to the discipline of architecture. Hadid's oeuvre in turn can be defined as an attempt to push ahead with "the incomplete project of modernism". This is the most general account Zaha Hadid has – on many occasions – given of her work. The "incomplete project of modernism", as Hadid understands it, is tilted more towards Russian Constructivism than German Functionalism, giving greater prominence to formal innovation than to scientific rationalization. But this opposition is one of degree rather than principle. For all shades of the modern movement, the historical intersection of abstract art, industrial technology and the social revolutions succeeding in the aftermath of the First World War have been the indispensable ingredients.

The introduction of categories such as "manifesto", "the discipline of architecture" and "oeuvre" suspends, but does not cancel or deny, concerns of utility. These categories are not set absolutely, autonomously and forever aloof from the functional concerns of society. Rather, the concrete uses and users are bracketed for the sake of experimenting with new, potentially generalizable principles of spatial organization and articulation with respect to emerging social demands and use patterns. Functional optimality according to well corroborated criteria is thus renounced for the experimental advancement of social practices of potentially higher functionality. The very nature of the kind of iconoclastic research of "the avant-garde" is that it thrusts itself into the unknown and offers its challenging proposals to the collective process of experimentation in a raw state, rather than waiting until the full cycle of experimentation, variation, selection, optimization and refinement is complete to present secure and polished results.

Despite the often precarious status of its partial and preliminary results, I will argue that this radicalism constitutes a form of research; an unorthodox research in as much as its methods include intuitive groping, randomization and automatic formal processes, i.e. the temporary relaxation and even suspension of rational criteria.

Post-modernism, Deconstructivism, Folding

Hegel grasped that the New in artistic and intellectual history is always consuming its immediate precursor as its defining opposite, maintaining and carrying it along like a shadow. And this shadow carries a further shadow etc., so that cultural innovation can only be identified and appreciated by those who are able to place it within the whole historical evolution. Such appreciation, therefore, becomes a relative, graded and ultimately infinite act. (And it is essential for the culture of architecture to insist that a new architectural position cannot be reduced to an isolated form or gesture, but – like a scientific idea – involves a whole network of historically cumulative assumptions and ambitions.) This process, which Hegel called *sublation*, is borne out by the fact that the definition of the New, e.g. of deconstructivism or folding in architecture, stretches across hundreds of magazine and book pages, broadly retracing architectural history, referencing classic as well as modernist tropes.

But – and this is beyond the grasp of Hegelian dialectic – each time the sequence is traversed it is twisted and retroactively realigned by current contingencies and emerging agendas. The history of (architectural) history reveals how distinctions and relative newness are redistributed, emerge and collapse under the force of current innovations and concerns, a force that thus works to a large extent against the arrow of time with bewitching consequences: a thought might no longer speak the language of its own beginning. As Derrida puts it "all is not to be thought at one go" and "the necessity of passing through that erased determination, the necessity of that trick of writing is irreducible" (Derrida 1974). However easy and natural the latest innovations (layerings, deformations) might seem to us now, they did constitute radical violations of the implicit rules of architectural order, and for the mainstream audience this oppositional character still dominates their perceived meaning. The innovative architect has no choice but to reckon and work with this dialectic determination by opposition or contrast. It will take time for the differences inherent to the new language to emerge from the shadow of the stark difference of new vs. old.

One argument here is that the current avant-garde language of architecture – with its incredible surge of creative energy and power,

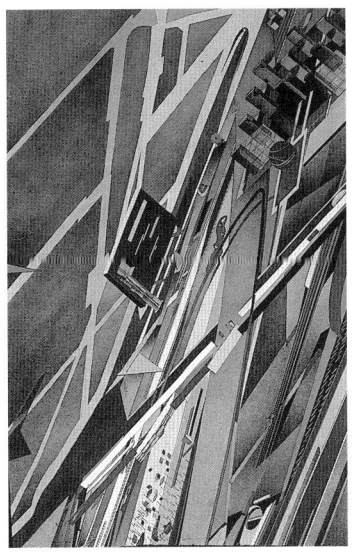

Parc de La Villette, Paris, 1982.

fuelled by the ongoing IT revolution – is conceptually still working out the ramifications of a series of dialectical reversals first launched by "deconstructivism". Further, we should not forget that the follow-on movement of "folding", too, was initially elaborated with pen and paper before it soaked up the new digital possibilities. Folding was counterposed to deconstructivism by a series of further reversals and oppositions – defined within the framework established by deconstructivism.
The rapid succession of these three movements within avantgarde architecture (1970s to 1990s) created the conceptual and formal resources from which the current digitally liberated work took off in the second half of the nineties. Venturi's *Complexity and Contradiction in Architecture*, and Colin Rowe's *Literal and Phenomenal Transparency* offered seminal conceptual innovations that can still guide ambitious design agendas today.
Peter Eisenman's method of transformational series, whereby he was working with series of successive over-determinations of an initial platonic primitive, anticipates the method the CAD-systems used in modeling 3D solids via the Boolean operations of addition, subtraction and intersection. Eisenman's process is explicating his complex compositions as the end result of an explicit and retrievable series of such operations. This is mirrored in the ability of the CAD-system to keep a retrievable record of the history of object construction. The designer is enabled to retrace his steps and intervene in the recorded history of design steps, and depending upon the combinatorial dependencies between operations, he can make alternative choices at any point in the sequence of over-determination. Eisenman was also the first – inspired by Colin Rowe's insightful analysis of Cubism – to employ the method of superposition of incongruent geometric organizations. The resulting accidental

clashes and interferences were cherished as interesting new compositional effects. It was Tschumi's contribution to foreground and radicalize this method most effectively in his seminal project for the Parc de La Villette in Paris. (The competition drawings were much more striking and influential than the built project, which took many years to complete.) This project stated the principle of layering with crystal clear radicality. Multiple, divers spatial reference systems were occupying the same site. However, at this stage in the development of a new language of spatial complexity, the layered spatial reference systems – point-grid, meandering line, system of platonic figures – were indifferent to each other. The layers are breaking through each other without registering each other. There is no mutual inflection, adaptation or any attempt at integration. This was first achieved by Zaha Hadid, who realized a seamless coherence in her complex and deep, pictorial textures. Even her contribution to the competition for La Villette already displays the seeds of these characteristics. The interarticulation of various spatial layers went hand in hand with the curve-linear distortion and dynamization of the complex spatial arrangements.

It was Jeff Kipnis' and Greg Lynn's contribution to elaborate the theoretical terms that allows us to focus our attention on these most advanced formal characteristics. Concepts like smooth vs. striated space (taken from Deleuze & Guattari's *Thousand Plateaus*), deformation as registration of programmatic and contextual information, multiple affiliation, and intensive coherence were offered as poignant descriptions and worthy ambitions. Greg Lynn soon moved ahead with the strategic deployment of brand new animation software tools to explore effective design techniques that could help to deliver the spatial qualities described in those concepts: meta-balls (=blobs), nurb meshes, inverse-kinematic skeletons etc.

Zaha Hadid Architects were quick to upgrade their digital toolkit to continue and intensify their exploration of dynamic and organically integrated complexity. In fact, even before these new software systems were brought in, Zaha Hadid Architects were already using the Xerox machine to partly mechanize some of the most pertinent design moves: smearing drawings across the Xerox machine following a curved or s-curved trajectory produced the desired dynamization and smoothing effects.

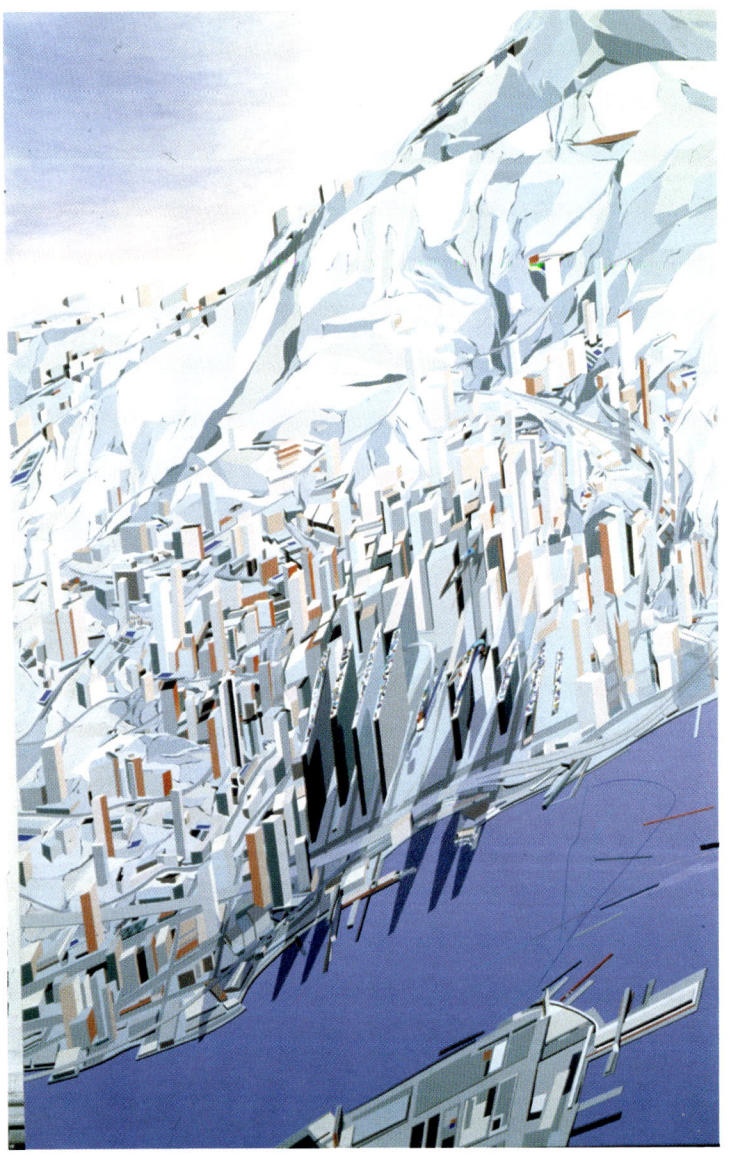

Hong Kong, The Peak, *1982. Next page: Vitra Fire Station, Weil Am Rhein, 1990-94.*

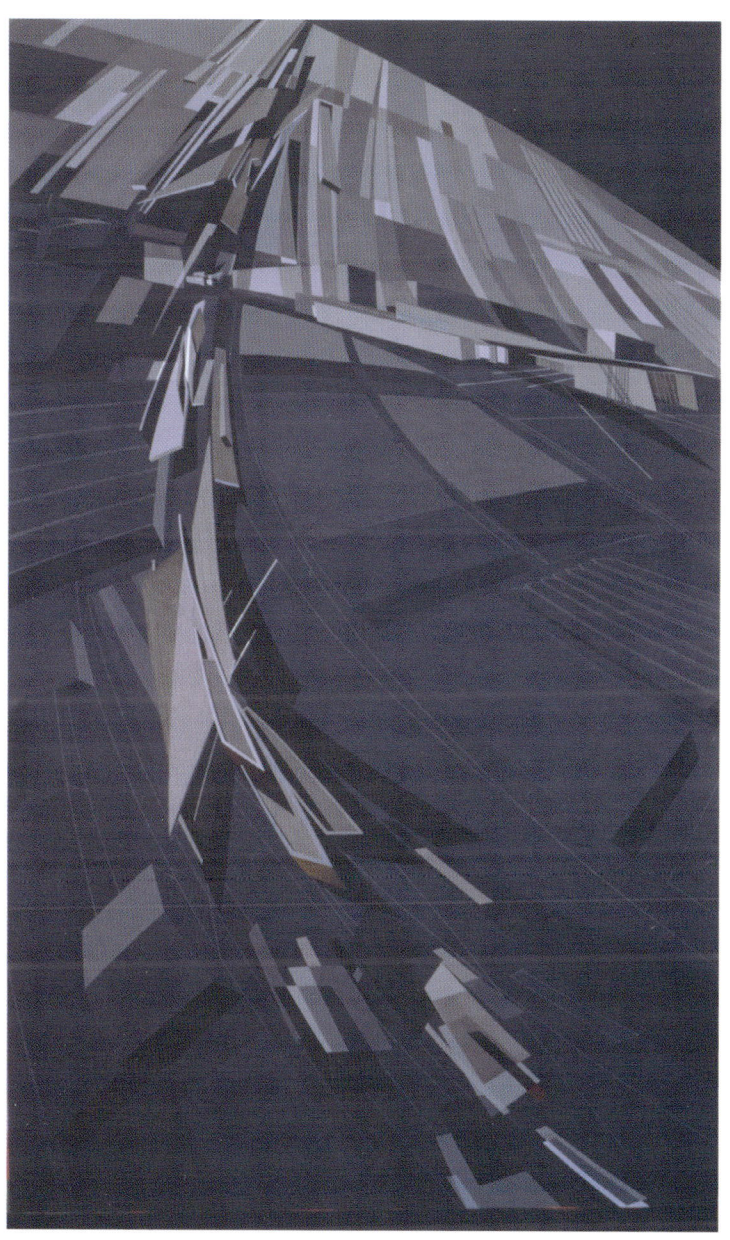

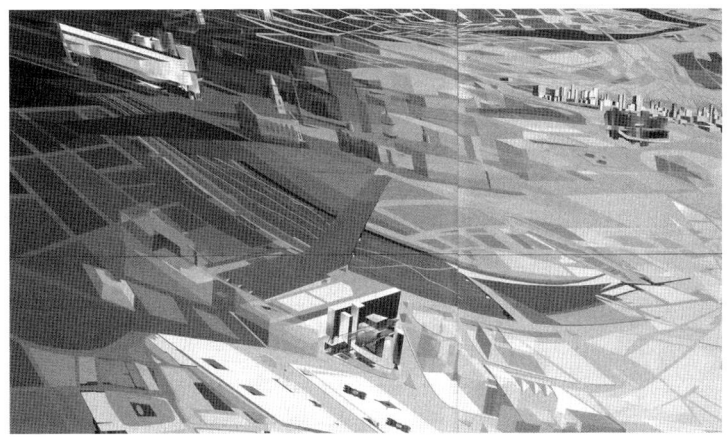

Grand Buildings, Trafalgar Square, London, 1985.

While it is important to reveal the genealogy of the formal and conceptual apparatus of the current architectural avant-garde (which includes Hadid as one of its practitioners and precursors), such a genealogy is not written in a spirit that wants to reduce what is going on now to what has been, or foreclose the current and future potential for developing the repertoire in new directions. That cannot be the purpose of *Digital Hadid*.

We have nearly reached the point in our argument where we have to pose the question – given this genealogy – what is fundamentally new now and what points towards further radical mutations of architecture in terms of its methods, concepts and forms. The best way to approach this question might be via a review of the most recent series of projects coming from Zaha Hadid Architects. However, before we do this we should make yet another short excursion into the methods and mechanisms of invention that have been prevalent in Hadid's previous work.

Mechanisms of Invention

RECOMBINATION: COLLAGE AND HYBRIDIZATION

A key mechanism that has to be mentioned here is the dialectic of recombination and hybridization. The important reminder

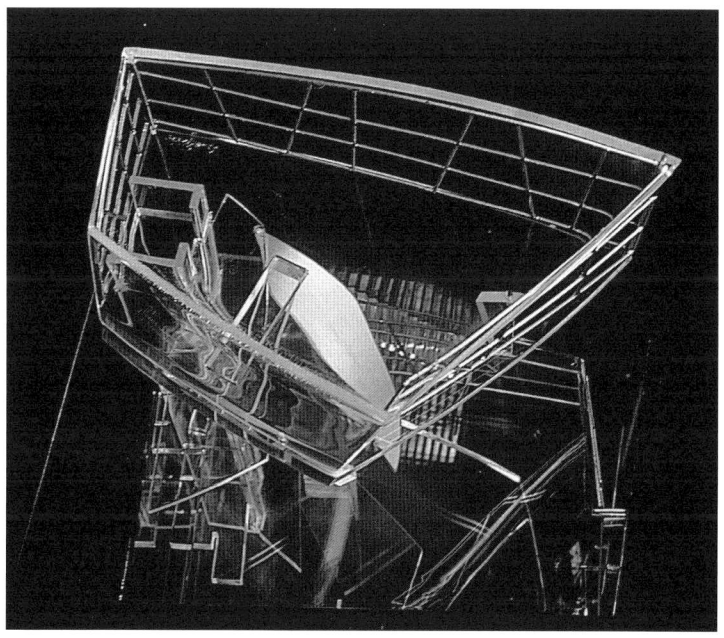

Azabu-Jyuban, Tokyo, 1986.

here is that the result of combination is rarely just a predictable compromise. Synergies might be harnessed: unpredictable operational effects might emerge and, on the side of meaning, effects are engendered as the whole taxonomy of differences is forced into an unpredictable realignment. The new combination re-contextualizes and reinterprets its ingredients as well as its surroundings. Currently, it is the various morphing tools that afford the most sophisticated form of formal hybridization, resulting in hybrids that appear as seamless wholes, leaving no trace of any conflicting figures in their origin. Kolatan & Macdonald focused attention on this form of hybridization, introducing the suggestive term *chimera* to denote the resultant effect.

ABSTRACTION
Abstraction implies the avoidance of familiar, ready-made typologies. Instead of taking for granted things like houses, rooms, win-

dows, roofs etc. Hadid reconstitutes the functions of territorialization, enclosure and interfacing etc. by means of boundaries, fields, planes, volumes, cuts, ribbons etc. The creative freedom of this approach is due to the open-endedness of the compositional configurations, as well as the open-endedness of the list of abstract entities that enter into the composition. To maintain the liberating spirit of abstraction, in the final building a defamiliarizing, "minimalist" detailing prevents volumes from immediately denoting rooms and cuts turn into windows again.

This minimalism withdraws the familiar items that otherwise would allow the inhabitants to fall into habitual patterns of behavior. Instead, they are confronted with an abstract composition that needs to be discovered and made sense of in a new way. Instead of points, lines, and planes we now work with control points, splines, nurb surfaces, and force-fields etc.

ANALOGIES

Analogies are fantastic engines of invention with respect to organizational diagrams, formal languages and tectonic systems. They have nothing to do with allegory or semantics in general. Hadid's preferred source of analogical transference is the inexhaustible realm of landscape formations: forests, canyons, river deltas, dunes, glaciers/moraines, faulted geological strata, lava flows etc. Beyond such specific formations, abstract formal characteristics of landscape in general are brought into the ambit of architectural articulation.

The notion of an artificial landscape has been a pervasive working hypothesis within Hadid's oeuvre from the Hong Kong Peak onwards. Artificial landscapes are coherent spatial systems. They reject platonic exactitude but they are not just any "freeform". They have their peculiar lawfulness. They operate via gradients rather than hard edge delineation. They proliferate infinite variations rather than operating via the repetition of discrete types. They are indeterminate and leave room for active interpretation on the part of the inhabitants.

Ultimately, anything could serve as analogical inspiration. Often such analogies come to be considered as the concept of the project: the Cardiff Opera House as an inverted necklace, the Copenhagen Concert Hall as a block of terrazzo, the Victoria and Albert Museum extension as 3D TV, i.e. a three-dimensional pixelation etc. Most recently, Zaha Hadid Architects are exploring the possibility of exploiting analogies with organic systems.

Surrealist mechanisms

Hadid's audacious move to translate the dynamism and fluidity of her calligraphic hand directly into equally fluid tectonic systems, her incredible move from isometric and perspective projection to literal distortions of space, from the exploded axonometry to the literal explosion of space into fragments, from the superimposition of various fisheye perspectives to the literal bending and meltdown of space etc. – all these moves resemble the illogical operations of the surrealists.

The initially "mindless" sketching of graphic textures (see Vitra sketches) in endless iterations operates like an "abstract machine", proliferating differences to select from. Once a strange texture or figure is selected and confronted with a programmatic agenda, a peculiar form-content dialectic is engendered. An active figure-reading mind will find the desired conditions but equally new desires and functions are inspired by the encounter with the strange configuration. The radically irrational and arbitrary detour ends up hitting a target.

This "miracle" can be explained by recognizing that all functionality is relative, that all well-articulated organisms have once been monstrous aberrations and might later seem crude and deficient – relative to other "higher" and more "beautiful" organizations. Before we dismiss arbitrary formalisms, we need to realize that all our time-tested typologies themselves adhere dogmatically to the arbitrary formalism of orthogonality and platonic simplicity, derived from the constraints of measuring, making and stabilizing structures handed down to us from a rather primitive stage of our civilization. To remain locked in within these figures at this time and age would be more than arbitrary. The only way out is through the radical proliferation and testing of other options. All points of departure are equally arbitrary until tested against presumed criteria. There is no absolute optimality. Every measure starts with a finite array of arbitrary options to compare, select from, adapt and thus work away from absolute arbitrariness. It is significant in this respect that the logic of evolutionary innovation starts with mutation: mutation, selection and reproduction. Hadid has been a vital engine of mutation with respect to the culture of architecture.

II. Current Work. Towards a New Digitally Based Architectural Language

The work presented and discussed here is a selection of projects of the last five years which demonstrate the increasing impact of the new 3D modeling and animation software on the development of a new language for architecture.
Starting with the seminal winning competition for the Italian Contemporary Arts Center in Rome – now on site – and ending with the design for a new Guggenheim museum in Taichung, Taiwan. This string of projects is a quest for an increasingly organic approach to the articulation of architectural space and form. The projects selected are those projects of Zaha Hadid Architects which strongly manifest this ambition towards a new organic language. The author of this book is also the co-designer of the string of projects featured here.

Organic Interarticulation

The analogy of building and organism is as old as the self-conscious discipline of architecture itself. Traditionally, the analogy focused on key ordering principles like symmetry and proportion. These principles were seen as integrating the various parts into a whole by means of setting those parts into definite relations. In this conception, the organism is approximating an ideal type which implies strict rules of arrangement and proportion for all parts. It also assumes a state of completeness and perfection. The organism is a closed form: nothing can be added or subtracted. The Palladian Villa is perhaps the best example of this idea of the organism as an ideal of perfect order.
Our projects remain incomplete compositions, more akin to the Deleuzian notion of assemblage than to the classical conception of the organism. Our concept of organic integration does not rely on such fixed ideal types. Neither does it presuppose any proportional system, nor does it privilege symmetry. Instead, integration is achieved via various modes of spatial interlocking, by formulating soft transitions at the boundaries between parts and by means of morphological affiliation. The parts or subsystems

that are brought together to form a larger organic whole do not remain pure and indifferent to each other, but are mutually adapting to each other. The extreme example of organic fusion is perhaps our design for the lounging environment Ice-storm. Here, a series of previously discreet elements are interarticulated by means of morphing them into a larger encompassing structure. In this fashion, everything becomes literally continuous – a seamless form that is modulated and transformed to join the exact sectional profile of the embedded furniture pieces or to establish something akin to key to keyhole relations.

Another example is our design for a new Guggenheim Museum in Taichung. Here, the two gallery wings are mediated by letting both meld into the central communication space, which itself is made continuous with the surrounding park-scape. All transitions are made smooth. Changes in surface material never coincide (reinforce) changes in geometry. There are no add-on parts that could easily be separated out of the overall composition. The ramps and paths are cuts and folds molded into the ground-surface as well as into the envelope of the building. The lattice of the roof bridging across the central public space between the two gallery wings is not a neutral grid but an irregular triangulation that is adapted to the wedge-shaped gap between the two wings. Those structural beams are formally affiliated to the pedestrian bridges that cross this canyon-space below. The glass-mullions of the roof glazing continue this game of triangulation on a smaller scale. The openings within the building envelope are not punched out as arbitrary shapes. Instead, the surface is spliced along its lines of least curvature to create louvered openings akin to gills that respect the integrity of the surface.

In the case of the project for a new Music Centre for the BBC in London, the openings are created like worm-holes by turning the surface inside out, so that the innermost surface of the very deep wall fuses with the outermost envelope.

In the case of the Florence Train station, the openings are as three-dimensional and curve-linear as the overall body of the building itself – and not the imposition of platonic figures on an otherwise organic form.

These various treatments of the problem of articulating openings within an envelope are examples of our concept of organic inter-articulation. In each case, the attempt is made to avoid an arbitrary interference or interruption of the envelope. Instead, the quest is to integrate the openings into the structural and tectonic system of the envelope. In a similar way, all compositions are seen as tasks for creative organic interarticulation. A refined organic architecture resists easy decomposition – a measure of its complexity.

CENTER FOR CONTEMPORARY ARTS, ROME

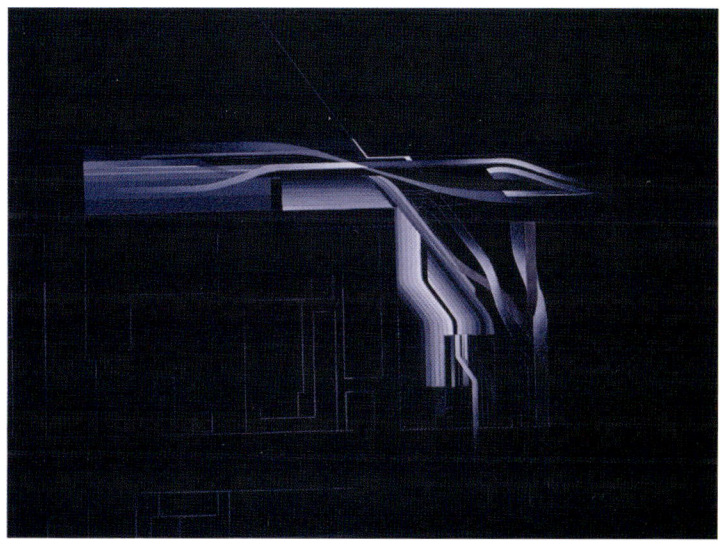

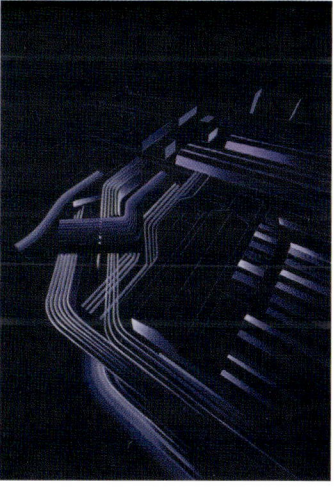

The Center for Contemporary Arts addresses the question of its urban context not by means of a stylistic pastiche but by an assimilation in terms of urban geometry. The project appears like an "urban graft", a second skin to the site. The initial design move was to flood the site with streams of parallel walls. Those walls variously converge and dissect, thus generating a pattern of interior and exterior spaces. The next step was to differentiate those walls into those bounding major linear spaces and those in between, which were lifted to become ribs structuring the roofs and ceilings of the major spaces. The result offers a quasi-urban field, a "world" to dive into rather than a building as a signature object. The Campus is organized and navigated on the basis of directional drifts and the distribution of densities rather than key points. This is indicative of the character of the Center as a whole:

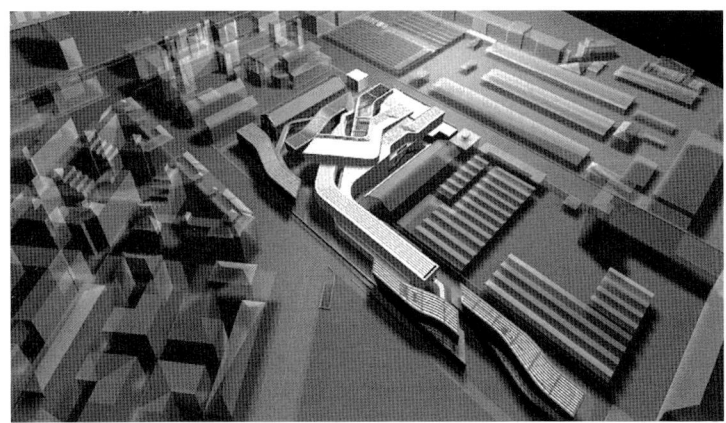

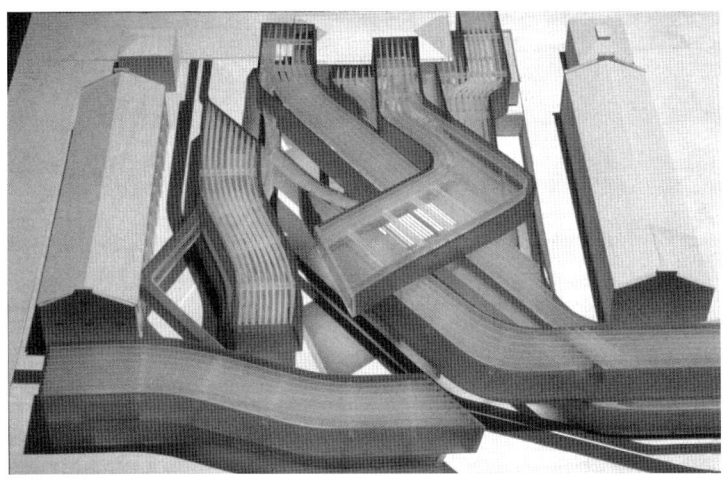

porous, immersive, a field space. An inferred mass is subverted by vectors of circulation. The external as well as internal circulation follows the overall drift of the geometry. Vertical and oblique circulation elements are located at areas of confluence, interference and turbulence. The premise of the architectural design promotes a disinheriting of the "object" orientated gallery space. Instead, the notion of a "drift" takes on an embodied form. The drifting emerges, therefore, as both architectural motif, and also as a way to navigate experientially through the museum. The "signature" aspect of an institution of this calibre is sublimated into a more pliable and porous organ-

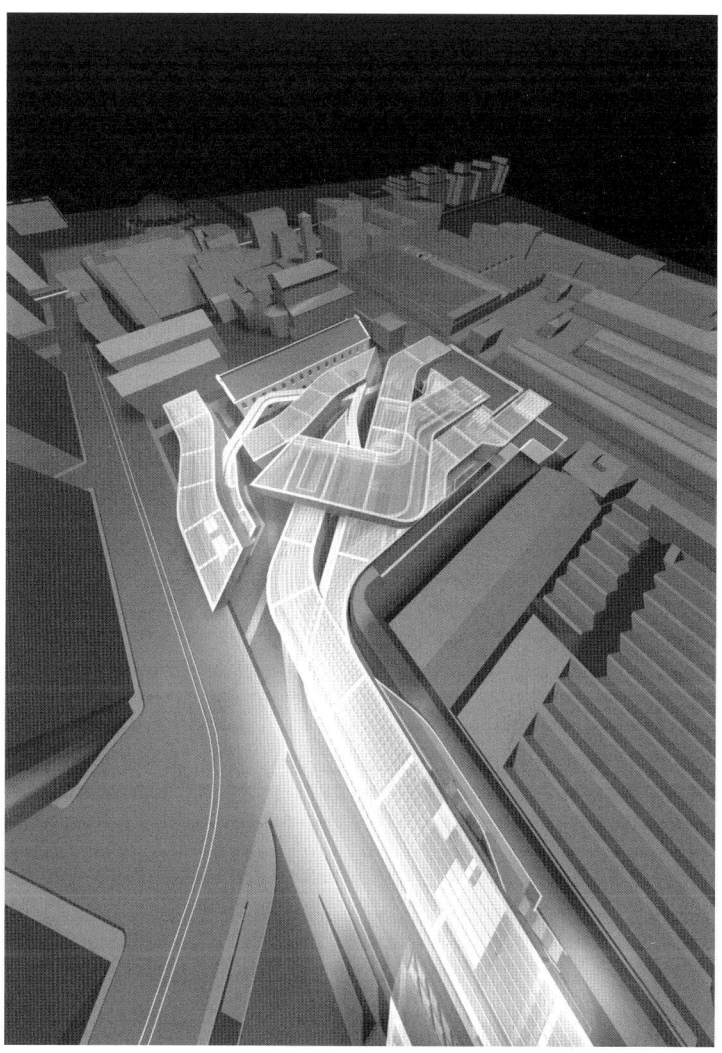

ism that promotes several forms of identification at once. In architectural terms, this is most virulently executed by the figure of the "wall". Against the traditional coding of the "wall" in the museum as the privileged and immutable vertical armature for the display of paintings, or delineating discrete spaces to construct "order" and linear "narrative", we propose a cri-

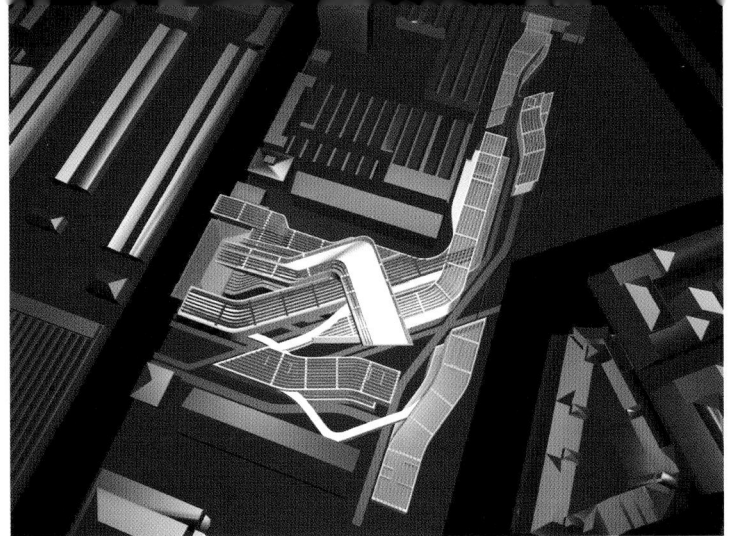

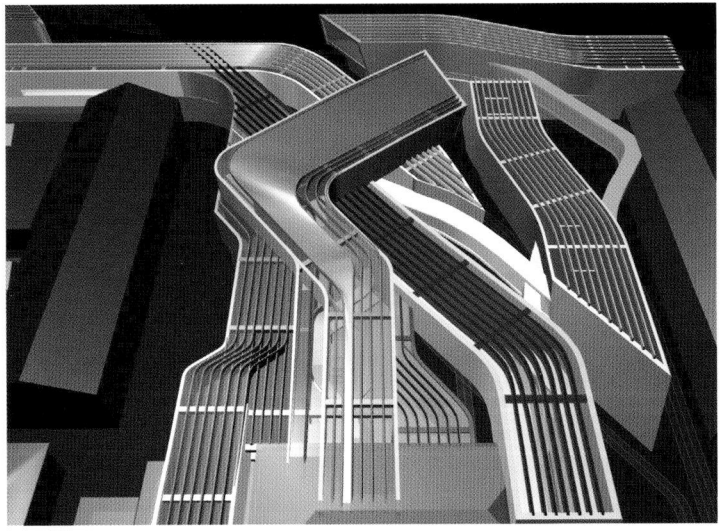

tique of it through its emancipation The "wall" becomes the versatile engine for the staging of exhibition effects. In its various guises – solid wall, projection screen, canvas, window to the city – the exhibition wall is the primary space-making device. By running extensively across the site, cursively and gesturally, the lines traverse inside and out. Urban space is coincidental with gallery space, exchanging pavilion and court in a continuous oscillation under the same operation. And further deviations from the classical compo-

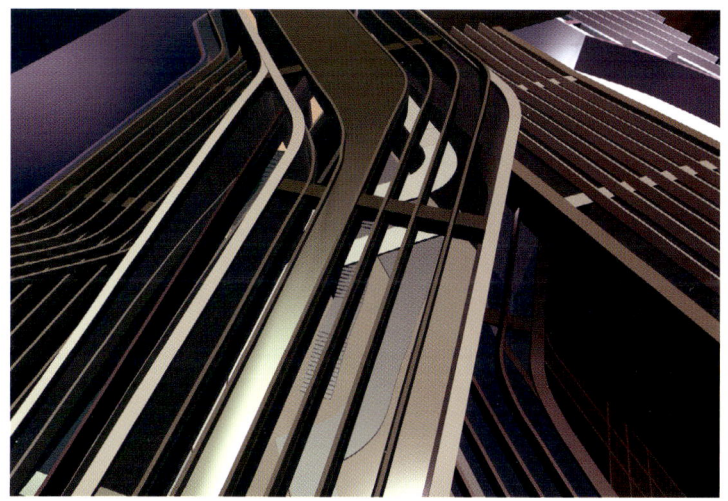

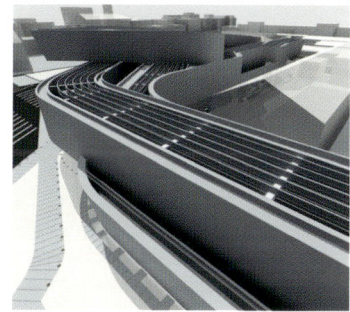
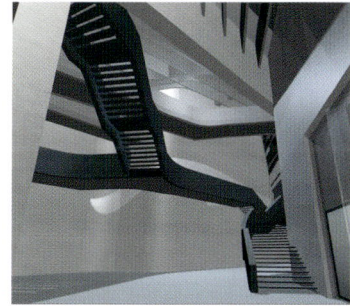

sition of the wall emerge as incidents where the walls become floor, or twist to become ceiling, or are voided to become a large window looking out. By constantly changing dimension and geometry, they adapt themselves to whatever curatorial role is needed. By setting within the gallery spaces a series of potential partitions that hang from the ceiling ribs, a versatile exhibition system is created. Organizational and spatial invention are thus dealt with simultaneously, amidst a rhythm found in the echo of the walls to the structural ribs in the ceiling that also filter the light in varying intensities. It is important to note that the whole project was initially composed of 2D splines and then crucially lifted into 3D (in 3ds max), where the integration between the primary levels was elaborated by means of voids, terracing galleries and ramps.

Art Center, Graz

The determining factor for the proposal was the desire to project and cantilever the building high over the street towards the riverbank. These considerations lead to the concept of a large canopy (raised 12m over the ground) that covers a tall volume of flexible space and acts as a large public room transparent and inviting. Arising from a forest of mushrooms, the canopy has a depth (height) varying between 3 to 6 metres. The underside is perhaps the strongest feature; the various structural stems bleed into the surface of the cantilevering volume. The composition was built up from contour lines and has been developed by a game of symmetry and deformation – creating figures of distorted symmetry. Its morphology is on the one hand derived from the urban context – as it was projecting

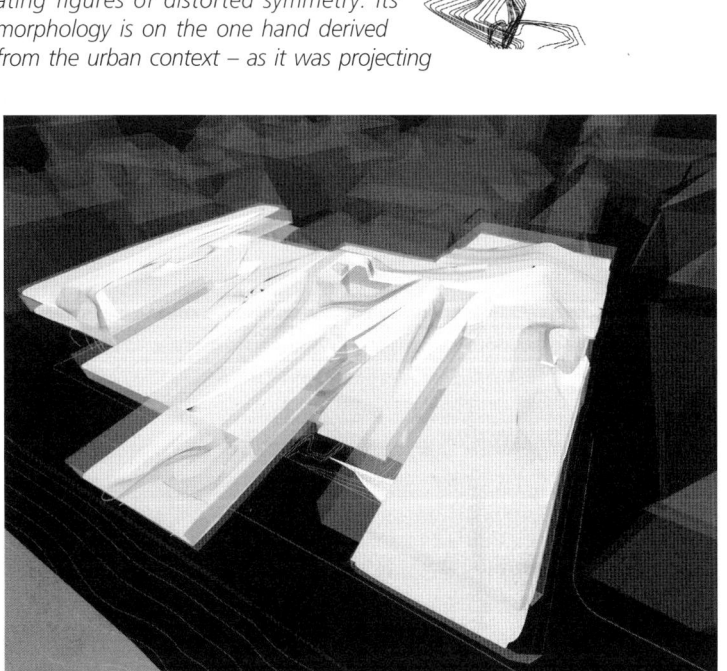

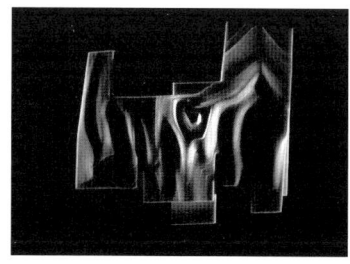

forward the profile of the existing fabric on the back of the site – and on the other, it has developed from the structural logic of the tapering mushroom columns. The art center is entered below the strongest cantilever. The main vertical circulation through the building moves through the hollow stem of the large mushroom. The volume below the canopy is a clear, open spatial expanse, which offers the lobby, commercial spaces and an exhibition area on the ground floor, as well as the flexible exhibition area on a flat level above ground. In contrast, the space within the canopy is enclosed, even compressed and highly articulated. It provides for those spaces which require intimacy, acoustic enclosure and darkness such as lectures and performances, the media center and the photography forum. The structure comprises inverted "trumpet forms" and cores organized to act as primary "inhabited" vertical supports. These forms are of reinforced concrete construction with doubly-curved surfaces to prevent deformation. The effect of splaying the fans out at the top allows large hoop tensions at the upper levels of the form, giving way to hoop compression at the bottom. The splays also assist in reducing the spans of the horizontal plates. The upper floors are interconnected with walls to allow the formation of a three-dimensional "vierendeel" structure with the horizontal plates acting as flanges. Cantilevers over the existing building and road are then made possible. The rigid horizontal form merges into the vertical fans with a seamless junction transferring vertical loads down to the ground.

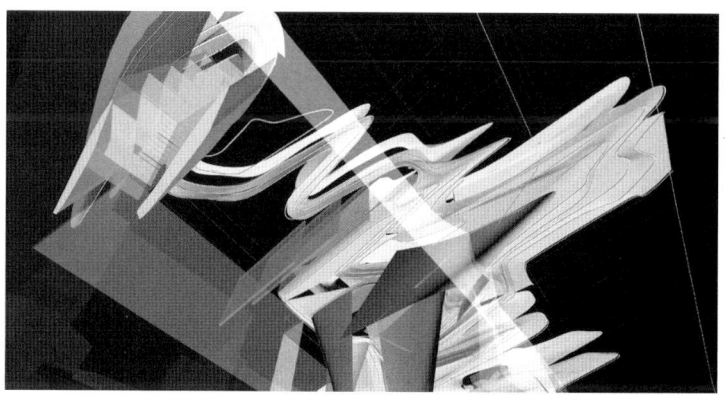

QUEBEC NATIONAL LIBRARY, MONTREAL

The overall massing proposed fills the urban block while leaving a well-sized urban plaza on the corner. The structuring of this mass emphasizes the pattern of public circulation through and within the building. A deep visual penetration of this mass is offered by means of deep cuts and crevices articulating access points as well as internal movements, revealing the manifold

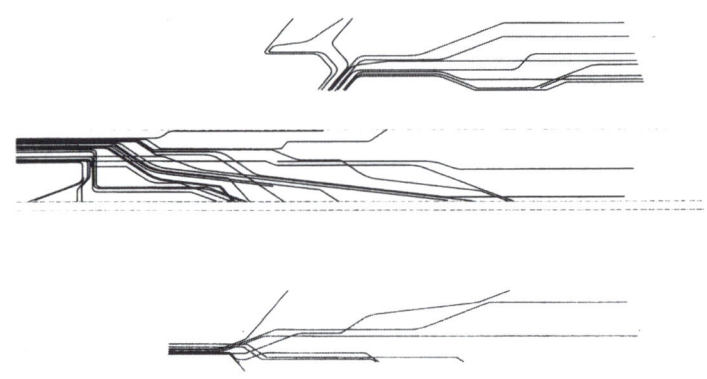

The tree of knowledge.

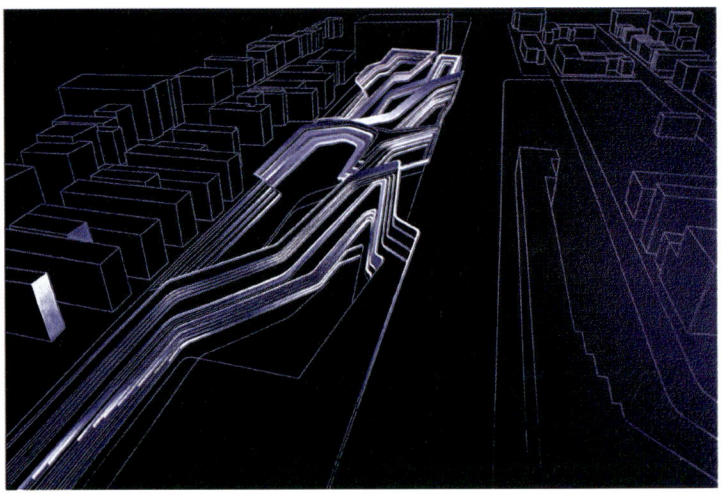

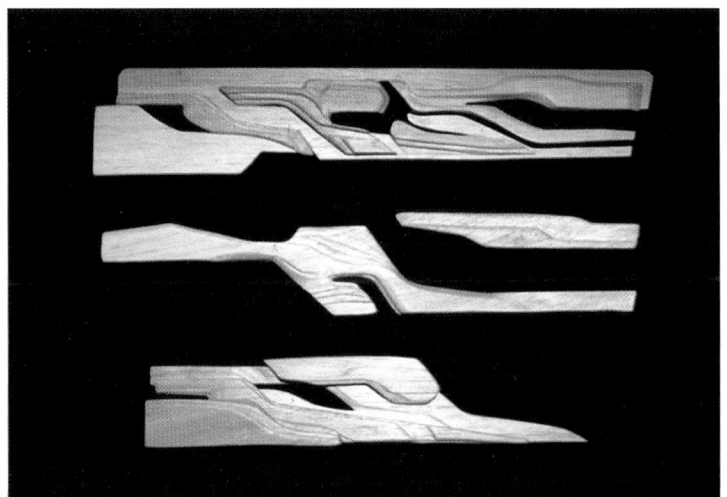

Models.

choreography of public events within the thick skin of the building. The two bulkheads of the site are articulated as public entrance rooms, piercing deep into the building. The main architectural concept is based on the articulation of a continuous navigation space that sequentially unfolds the various bodies of human knowledge contained in the different collections of the library. This navigation space follows the branching logic of successive disciplinary differentiation – the tree of knowledge. The navigation space is architecturally expressed as the veins eroding the solid mass of the building. The actual circulation through the building traces these voids and crevices, allowing for diagonal vistas and good orientation across levels. In this microcosm, the various channels of connection between the parts must be an active,

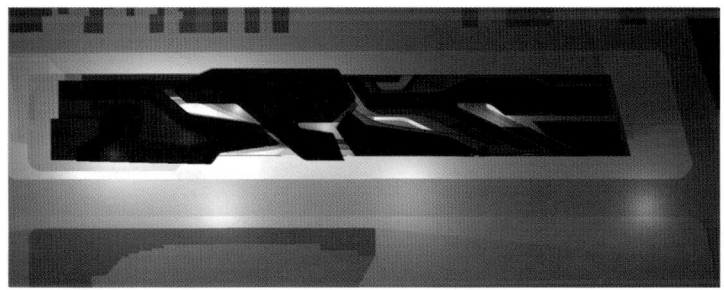

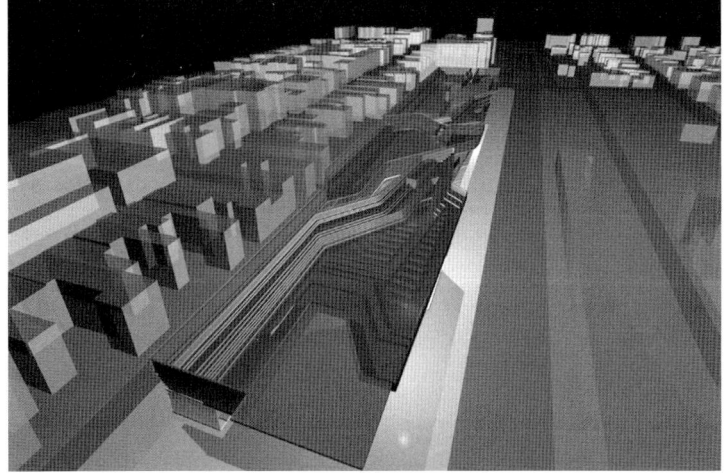

catalytic tissue within the library as a whole. The mass that is withstanding the erosion are the collection spaces filled with books and the reading rooms. The overall formation of this mass is undercut like an overhanging cliff exposed to view at the main entrance. This way, a main public void is created at the front of the building, offering the visitor revealing glimpses of the successive strata of the library. The visitor can follow the branching veins upwards before choosing his or her trajectory to the collections and reading rooms. The major collections are shaped like terraced valleys lined with books on the perimeter and the reading areas in the middle. The terracing offers differentiation as well as overall orientation. The reading rooms at the top of the building take advantage of the possibility of filtered daylight from above. The predominant interior material here is wood, providing intimacy and quietude. Atmospherically, these rooms are conceived in analogy with the canopy level of trees. The overall spatial organization is treated as a three-dimensional information design utilizing the ramifying pattern of the classification tree as a circulation diagram. The system of paths thus successively bifurcates according to the branches of human knowledge. This is also the path from the general to the particular. The more general information like the news library and encyclopedias are followed by the major division of human knowledge into the humanities and arts on the one hand and the hard sciences on the other. Each has its own root and trunk on the ground floor and ramifies upwards into the building like two intertwining trees. The humanities bifurcate into the arts (including music and literature) on the one hand and history and the social sciences on the other. The hard sciences branch into natural science vs. applied science or technology. The natural sciences are further differentiated into life sciences vs. physics etc. But this linear system of ramification is only the most basic backbone and point of departure for a whole series of overlaps, crossovers and lateral connections – e.g. economics is an important field of conversion and intersection between

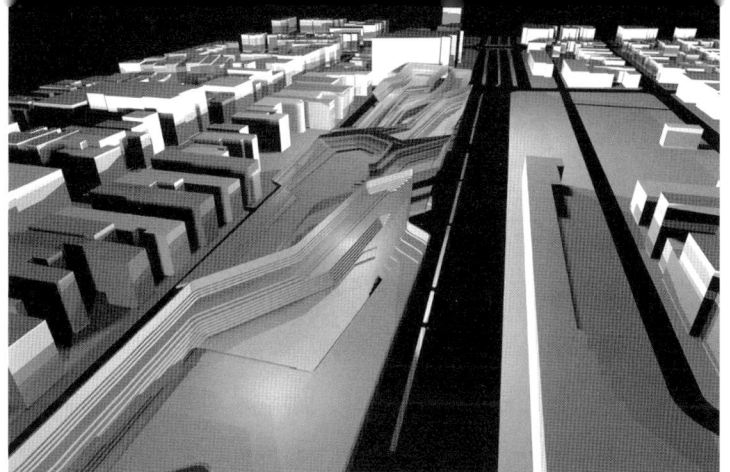

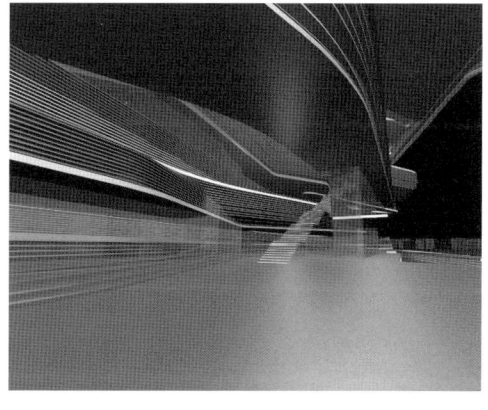

the humanities and hard sciences. The system becomes a network of multiple paths which allows for explorative browsing while the primary distinctions give an orienting armature to the increasingly complex labyrinth. The structure should underline the organizational logic of the library and reinforce the oblique trajectories through the building. Therefore, we suggest utilizing the necessary division walls as primary structural elements. These primary elements also orient the flows through the building. The structure is primarily constituted from interlocking structural walls. These walls do not need to line up vertically but rather act as transfer beams, they criss-cross and brace each other, forming a stiff three-dimensional lattice. This allows for the major spans which give the building its sense of generosity. The structural walls are selectively constructed in concrete or steel, as appropriate. Concrete dominates in the lower part of the building, while steel is introduced as cantilivering increases towards the top. There is a transition from the heavy base to a lighter top, gaining the benefit of the strength to weight ratio offered by steel construction. The top floor is very light in atmosphere. Here, the larger cantilivers project across the crevices and the roof plane should be porous to allow natural light to filter through.

ONE NORTH MASTERPLAN, SINGAPORE

The possibility of an urban architecture that exploits the spatial repertoire and morphology of natural landscape formations has been a consistent theme within the creative career of Zaha Hadid Architects for nearly 20 years. Indeed, our first moment of international recognition was already informed by a productive analogy with landscape conditions, here with geological form: the winning competition entry for the Hong Kong Peak in 1982. Our

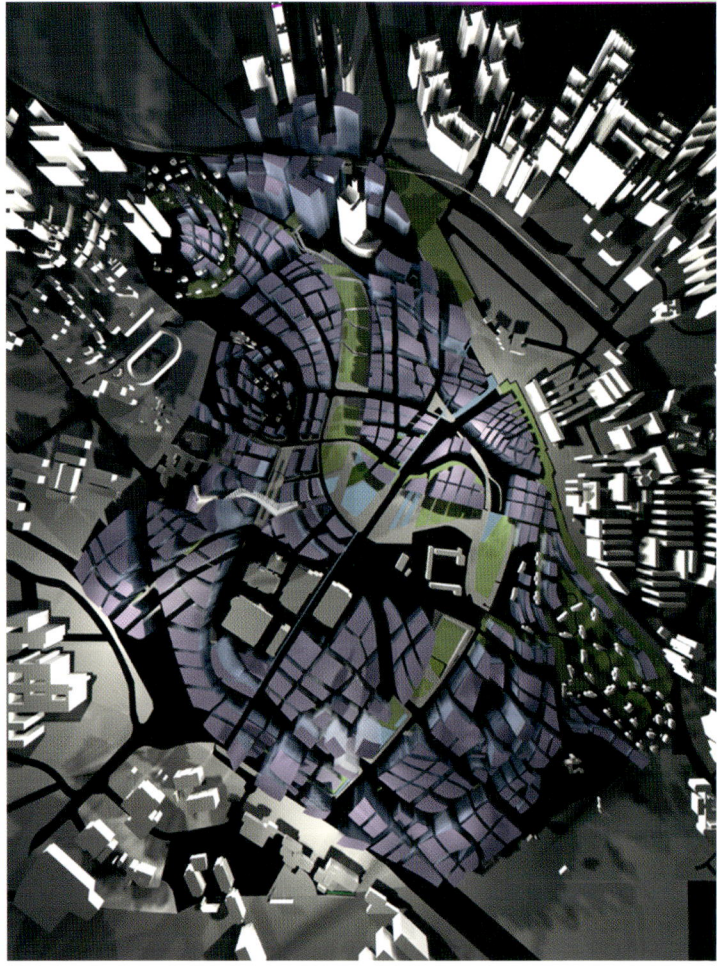

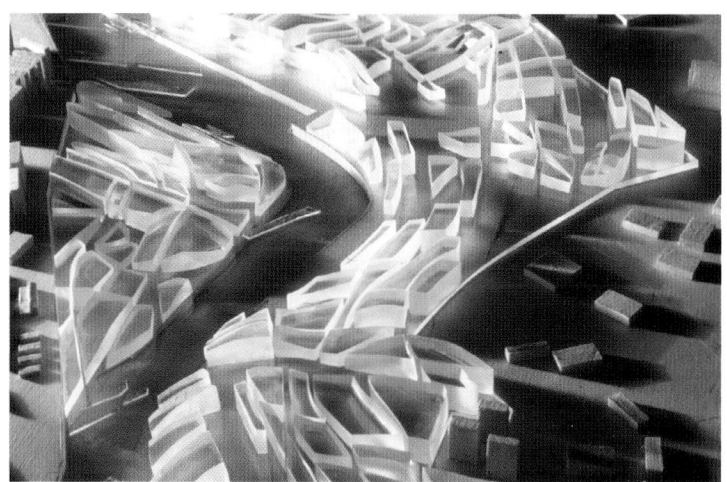

proposal for the Vista masterplan – for the first time – applies the concept of artificial landscape formation to the articulation of a whole urban quarter. The advantages of such a bold move are striking. Our scheme offers an original urban skyline and identifiable panorama visible from without as well as from the park in the heart of the new urban quarter. The rich diversity of squares and alleys engenders a unique sense of place within the various micro-environments. The concept of the gently undulating, dune-like urban mega-form gives a sense of spatial coherence that has become rare in the modern metropolis. The regulation of the building heights is a normal planning procedure and easily instituted. The powerful aesthetic potential that lies dormant in this ordinary planning tool has never been exploited before. An unusual degree of aesthetic cohesion and unity is achieved by allowing the roof surfaces to join in the creation of softly modulated surfaces. At the same time, a huge variety of built volumes – tall, low, wide, small – is brought under the spell of two unifying forces: the soft grid and the undulating roofscape. The softly swaying pattern of lines that defines the streets and paths, as well as the built fabric, allows the mediation and integration of the various heterogenous urban grids of the adjacent areas. The curve-linear pattern is able to absorb and harmonize all the divergent contextual orientations. It is also a machine to produce a huge diversity of building footprints without giving up on alignment from building to building. The morphological system allows for infinite variation within the bounds of a strong formal coherence and lawfulness. This is the great advantage of working with a "natural" geometry rather than with a strict platonic geometry. The form is "free" and therefore malleable at any stage of its development, while platonic figures (squares, circles,

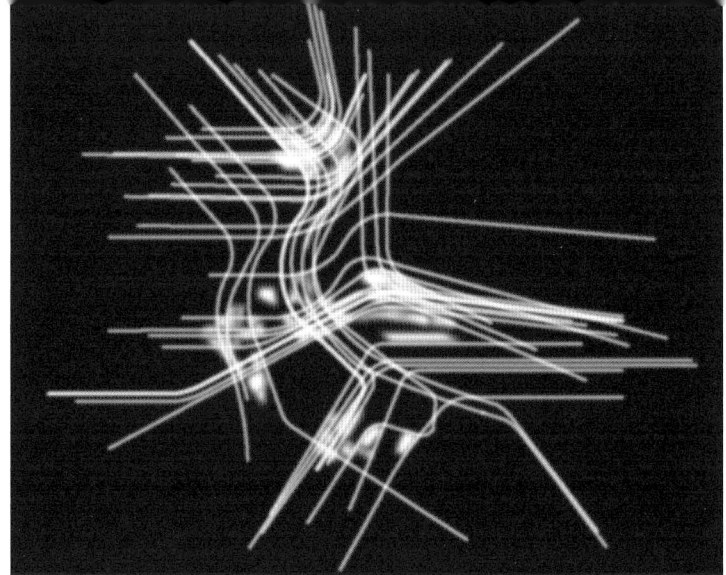

strict axes etc.) are too exacting and therefore vulnerable to corruption and degradation by later adaptations. The morphology is no less lawful and cohesive than the platonic system; but it is much more pliant and resilient, always able to absorb adaptations into its characteristic and recognizable form – always maintaining its coherence and character. The idea of an artificial landscape formation occurs not only on the level of the overall urban form. Not only the mega-form but also some of the micro-environments could benefit from the landscape analogy. In particular, we are thinking about the hub areas. One of the possibilities of developing the hub areas could be to introduce a raised plaza level about 5 meters above the street level. These raised grounds will be connected to the ground proper through the interiors of the buildings, as well as by means of broad staircases and shallow ramps on the exterior. Within the oeuvre of Zaha Hadid Architects there is a long series of urban schemes which explore various artificial landscapes as a means to sculpt public space and to impregnate it with a public program. These schemes manipulate and multiply the ground surface by sloping, warping, peeling or terracing the ground. Important advantages may be achieved by such manipulation. The visual orientation within the public realm is enhanced by tilting the plane into view and allowing for vistas overlooking the scene from above. By means of a gentle differentiation of slopes, ridges, terraces etc., the ground plane can be used to choreograph and channel movements across the plane in an unobtrusive and suggestive manner. The landscaped surface is rich with latent places. Articulations like shallow valleys or hills might give a foothold to gatherings and become receptacles for outdoor events without otherwise predetermining or obstructing the field.

BMW Plant - Central Building, Leipzig

The Central Building is the active nerve centre or brain of the whole factory complex. All threads of the building's activities gather together and branch out again from here. This planning strategy applies to the cycles and trajectories of people – workers (arriving in the morning and returning for lunch) and visitors – as well as for the cycle and progress of the production line which traverses this central point - departing and returning again. This dynamic focal point of the enterprise is made visually evident in the proposed dynamic spatial system that encompasses the whole northern front of the factory and articulates the central building as the point of confluence and culmination of the various converging flows. It seems as if the whole expanse of this side of the factory is oriented and animated by a force field emanating from the central building. All movement converging on the site is funneled through this compression chamber squeezed between the three main segments of production: Body in White, Paint Shop and Assembly. The primary organizing strategy is the scissor-section that connects ground floor and first floor into a continuous field. Two sequences of terraced plates – like giant staircases – step up from north to south and from south to north. One commences close to the public lobby passing by/overlooking the forum to reach the first floor in the middle of the building. The other cascade starts with the cafeteria at the south end moving up to meet the first cascade then moving all the way up to

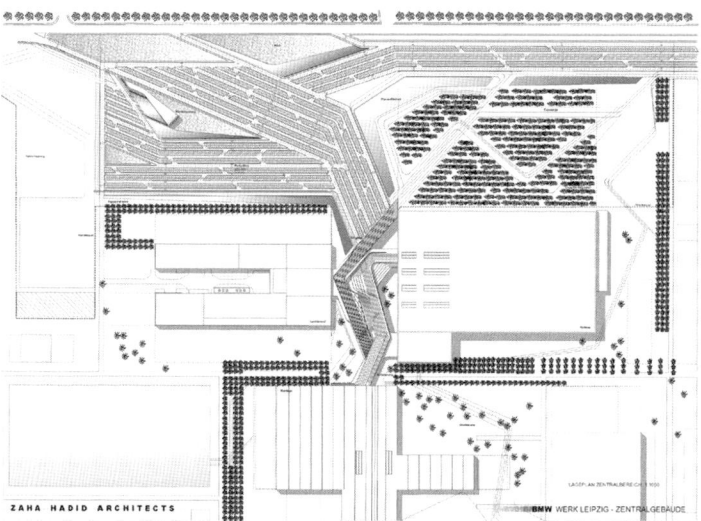

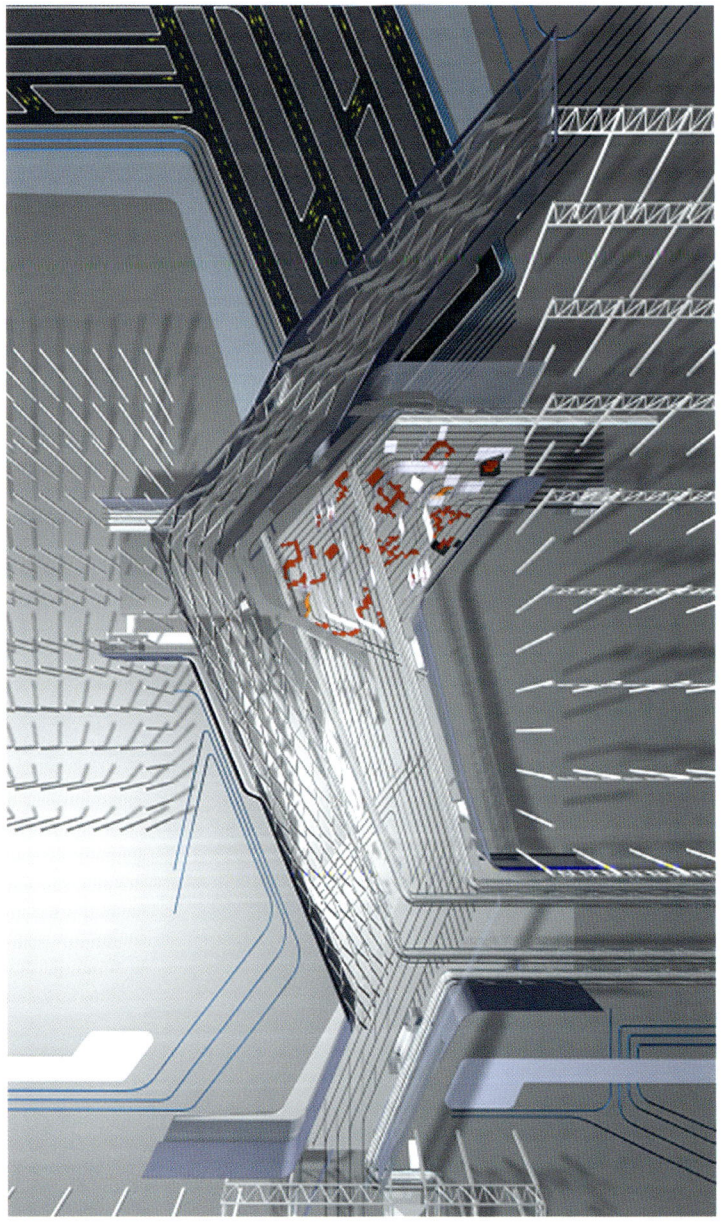

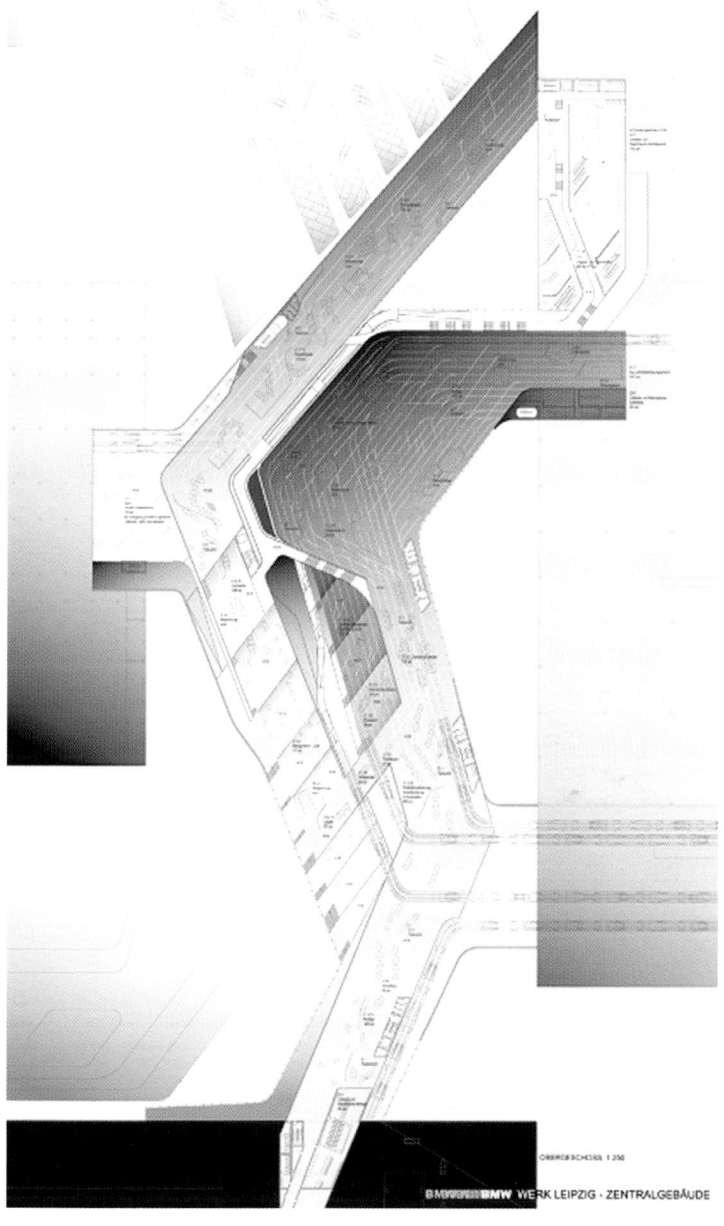

OBERGESCHOSS 1:250

BMW WERK LEIPZIG · ZENTRALGEBÄUDE

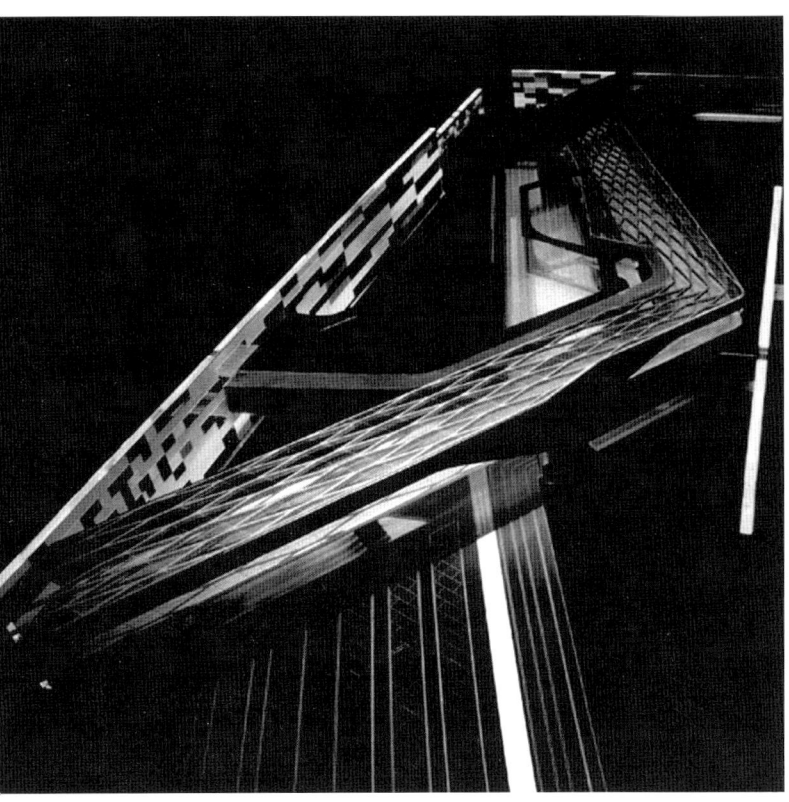

the space projecting over the entrance. The two cascading sequences capture a long connective void between them. At the bottom of this void is the auditing area as a central focus of everybody's attention. Above the void, the half-finished cars are moving along their tracks between the various surrounding production units that are open to view. The cascading floor plates are large enough to allow for flexible occupation patterns. The advantage lies in the articulation of recognizable domains within an overall field. Also, the global field is opened up to visual communication much more than would be possible on a single flat floorplate. The close integration of all the workers is facilitated by the overall transparency of the internal organization. The mixing of functions avoids the traditional segregation into status groups that is no longer conducive to a modern workplace. A whole series of engineering and administrative functions are located within the trajectory of the manual workforce coming in to work or moving in and out of their lunch break. White col-

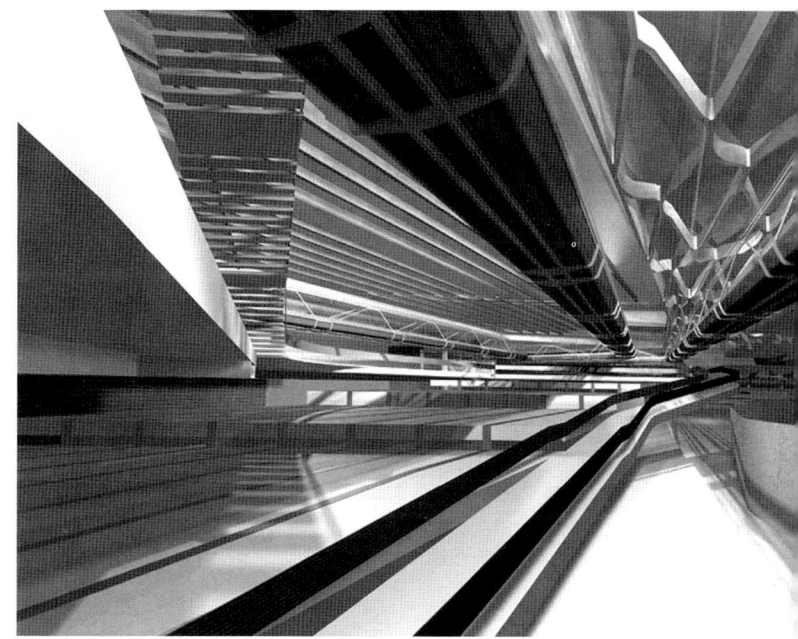

lar functions are located both on the ground floor and the first floor. Equally, some of the blue collar spaces (lockers and social spaces) are located on the first floor. This way, the establishment of exclusive domain is prevented. The potential problem of placing a large car park in front of the building had to be turned into an integral architectural feature that carries the scheme by turning it into a dynamic spectacle in its own right. The inherent dynamism of vehicle movement and the "lively" field of the car bodies is revealed by giving the arrangement of parking lots a twist that lets the whole field move, colour and sparkle. The swooping trajectories across the field culminate within the building. The architecture we are developing is no longer the architecture of repetition and pre-conceived forms. Rather, it is an organic architecture that is able to adapt and mould itself to the peculiarities of the terrain, to orient itself to the various directions of access and to synthesize a complex series of concerns into a seamless and integrated whole. This is made possible by the curve-linear morphology that can incorporate a multitude of forms and directions without fragmentation. New, numerically controlled manufacturing techniques make this quasi-natural process of formal variation possible and affordable. The result is aiming to come closer to the compelling beauty of living organisms.

ICE-STORM, LOUNGING ENVIRONMENT

Ice-storm *is an installation that was conceived and created for the Museum of Applied Arts (MAK) in Vienna. It is a built manifesto towards the potential for a new domestic language of architecture, driven by the new digital design*

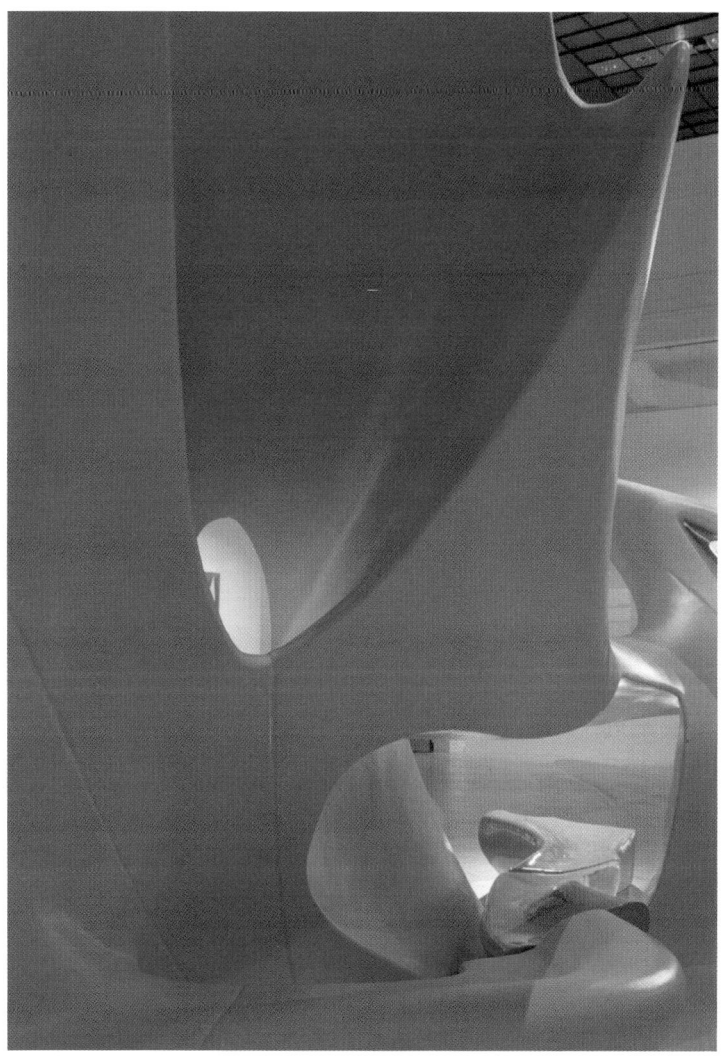

and manufacturing capabilities. The installation is suggestive of new types of living/lounging environments. In this respect, it is a latent rather than manifest environment. Neither familiar typologies nor any codes of conduct are yet associated with its morphology. The installation collects and fuses a series of previously designed furniture elements and installations: Glacier, Moraine,

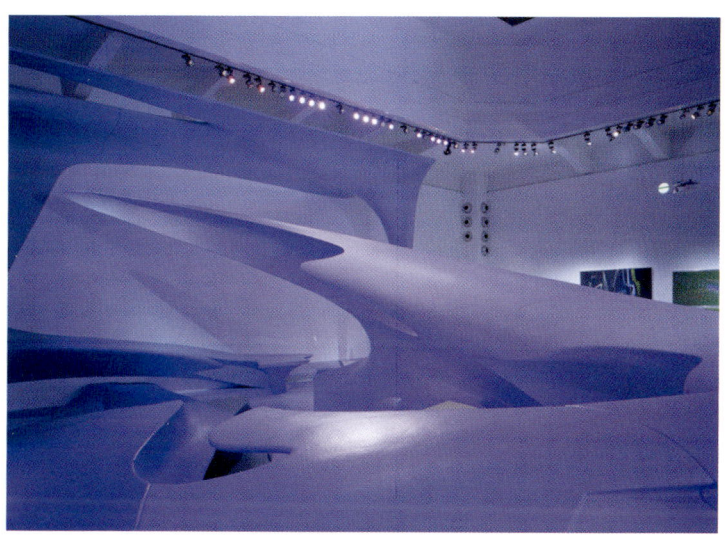

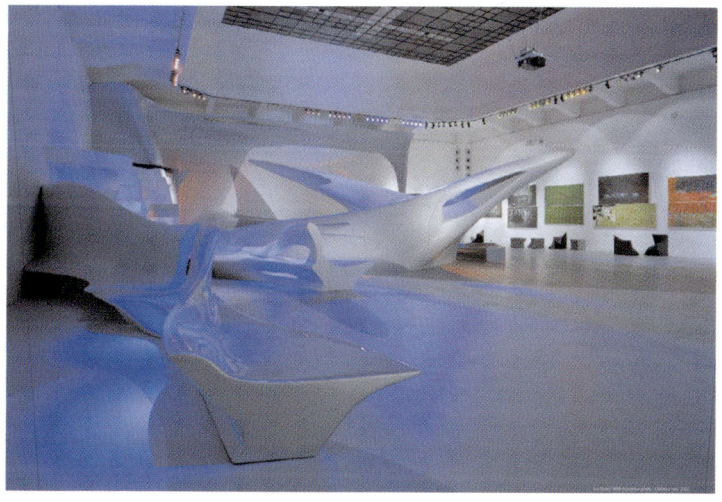

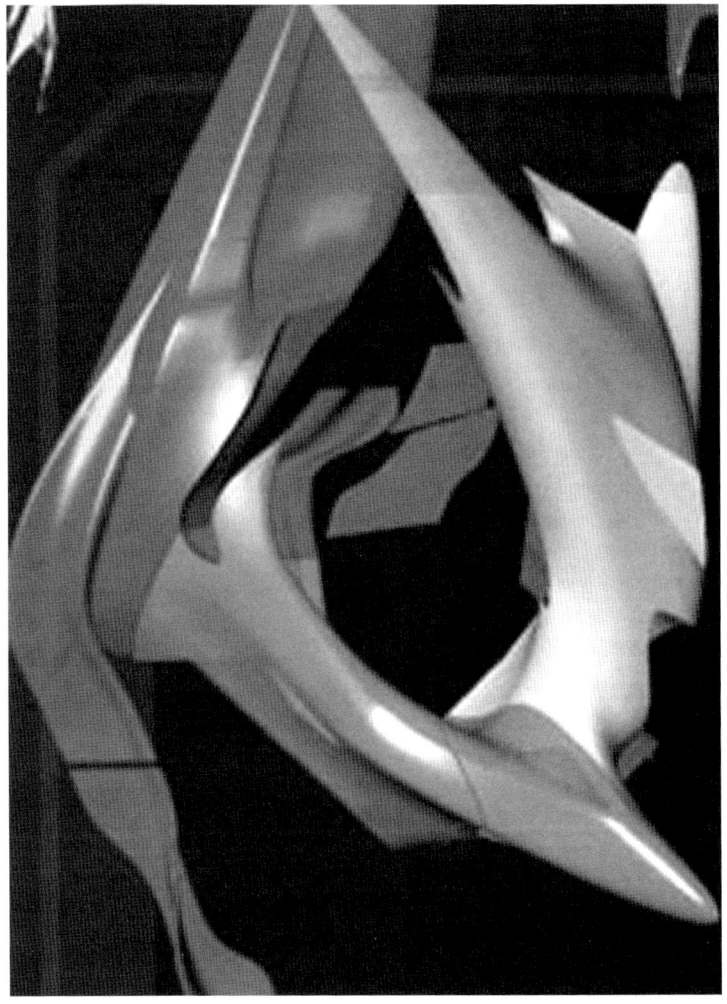

Stalactite, Stalagmite, Ice-berg, Z-Play and Domestic Wave including Ice-flow. These divers elements are drawn into a dynamic vortex. In addition, two new hard sofas have been designed to be integrated into the installation. The semi-abstract, molded surface might be read as an apartment that has been carved from a single continuous mass. The rhythm of folds, niches, recesses and protrusions follows a willful formal logic. This formal dynamic has been triggered by a series of semi-functional insertions which hint at the potential

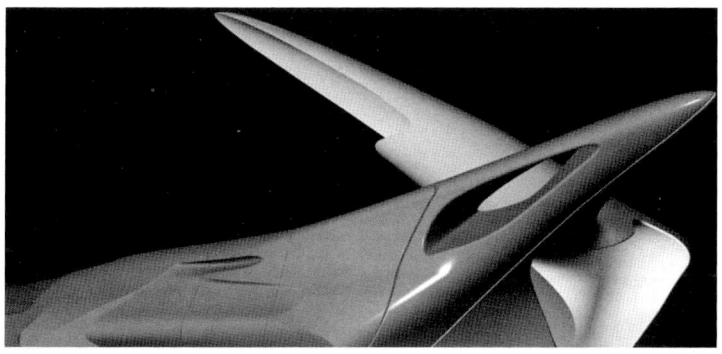

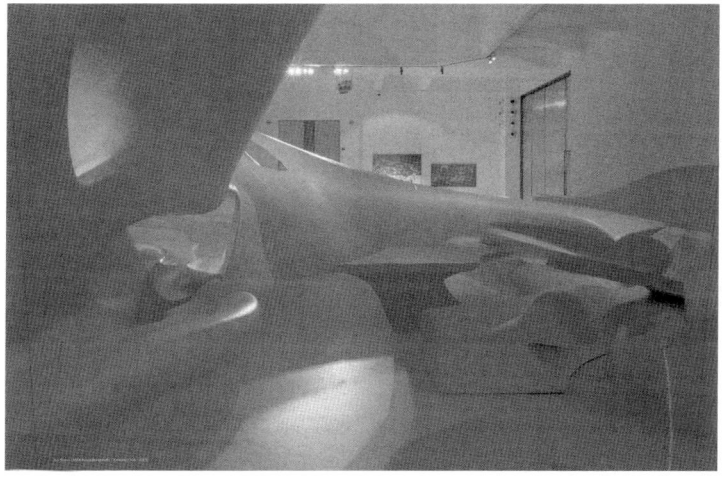

for sofas, day-beds, desks, tables etc. The design language explored here emphasizes complex curve-linearity, seamlessness and the smooth transition between otherwise disparate elements. This formal integration of divers forms has been achieved by the technique of "morphing". Via this morphing operation, the pre-existing furniture pieces are embedded within the overall fluid mass of the ensemble and become integrated organs of the overall organism. Those elements which are not contiguous with the overall figure – the Z-Play pieces – are nevertheless morphologically affiliated and appear like loose fragments that drift around the scene at random. The installation asks the visitors to occupy the structure and to explore for themselves this new, open aesthetic, which invites us to reinvent ourselves in terms of posture, demeanor and life-style.

Z-SCAPE, LOUNGING FURNITURE

Z-scape *is a compact ensemble of lounging furniture for public and private living rooms. The formal concept is derived from dynamic landscape formations like glaciers and erosions. The different pieces are constituted as fragments determined by the overall mass and its diagonal veins. Along these veins the block splits, offering large splinters for further erosive sculpting. Four pieces have emerged so far: Stalactite, Stalagmite, Glacier, Moraine.*

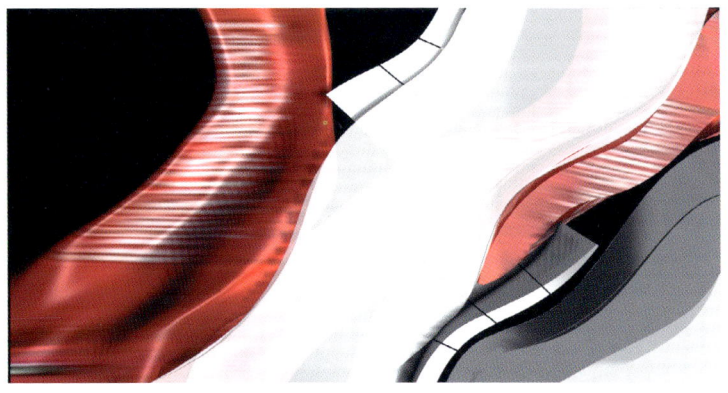

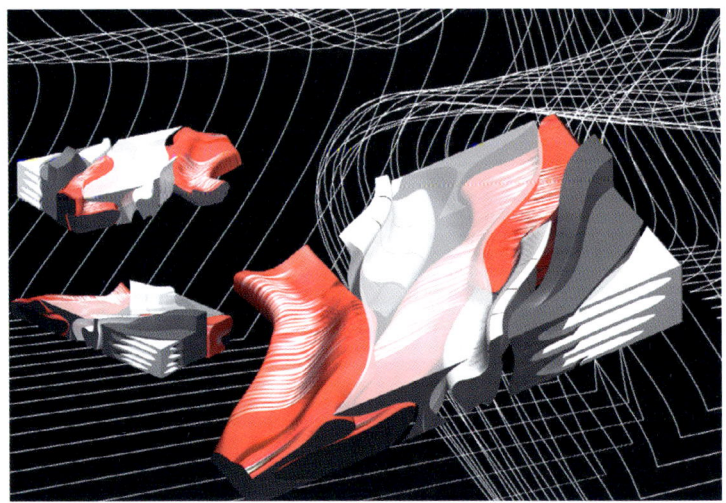

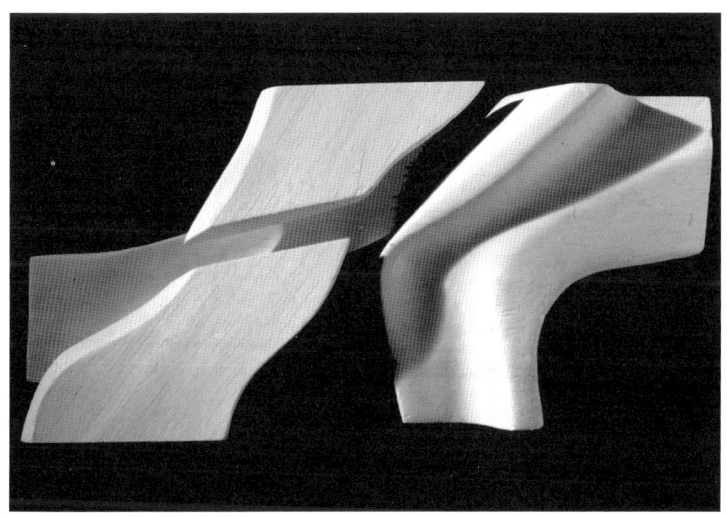

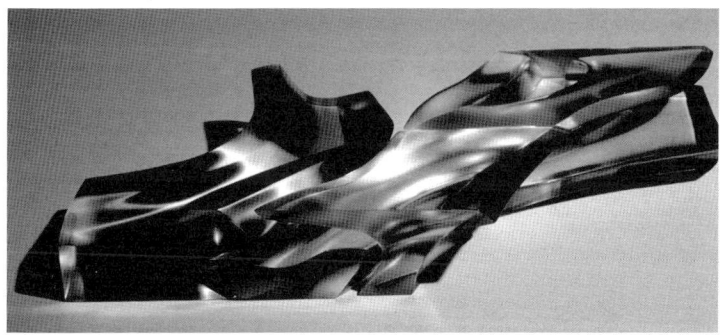

Others are yet to be unearthed. The pieces thus derived are then further shaped – if rather loosely – by typological, functional and ergonomic considerations. But these further determinations remain secondary and precariously dependent on the overriding formal language. We do not want to offer optimized and thus predetermined use-patterns. A margin of strangeness and indeterminancy is desired. Stimulation emerges between abstraction and metaphor.

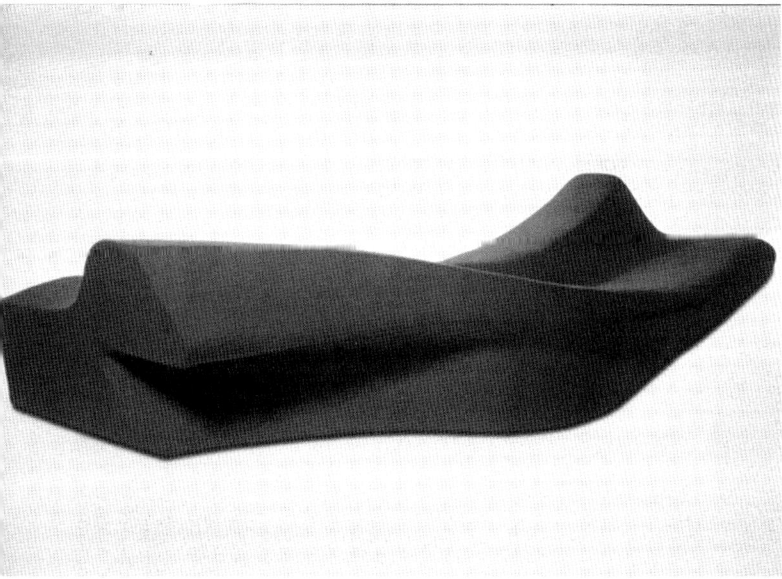

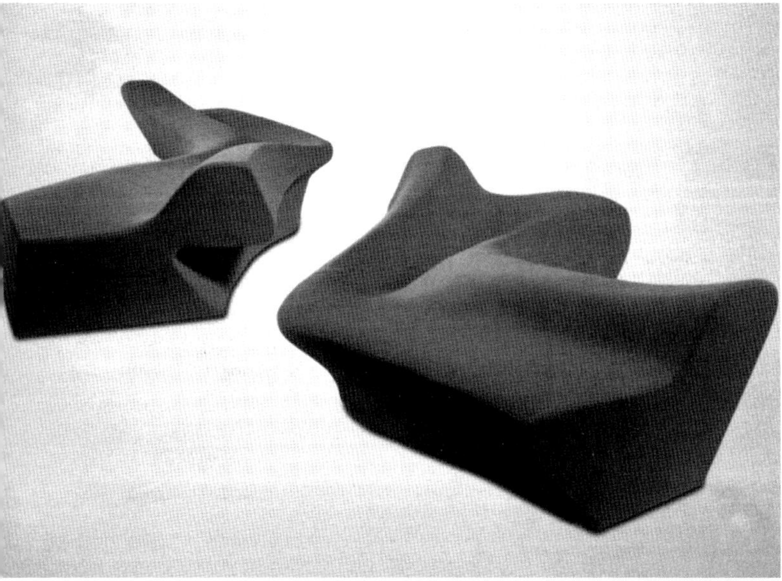

58

BBC Music Centre and Offices, London

The design task is the creation of a powerful landmark building acting as an iconic gateway into the BBC White City Campus. The key challenge we face as designers in this respect is the fact that this landmark is to be composed of two separate components with rather different functions: the BBC Music Centre on the one side and an office building – that might or might not be occupied by the BBC itself – on the other side. A further difficulty is that the two components may not be constructed at the same time. Therefore, independent successive construction needs to be possible. Given that the office

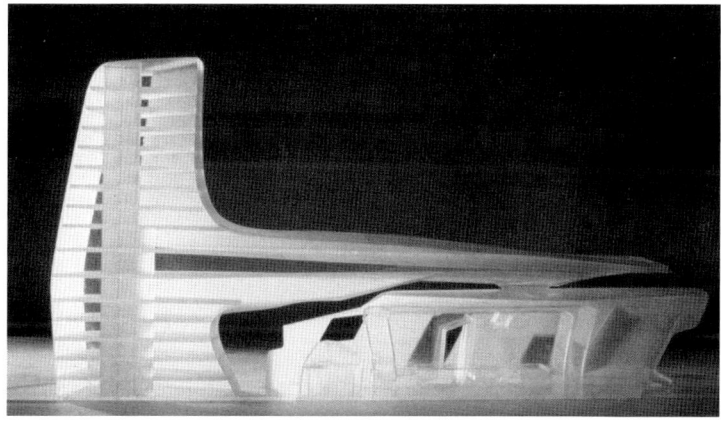

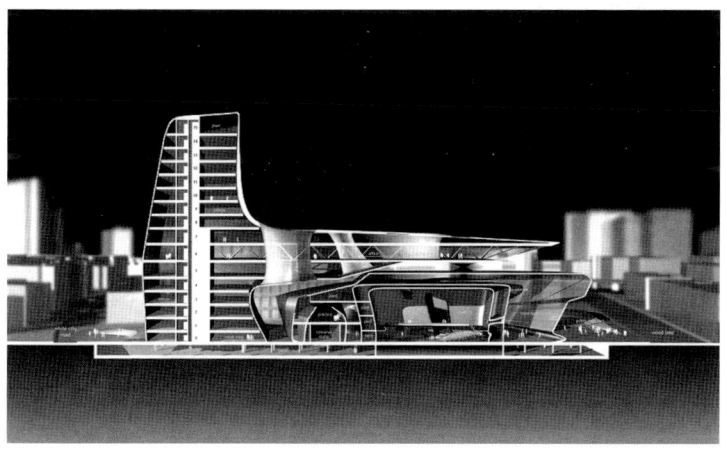

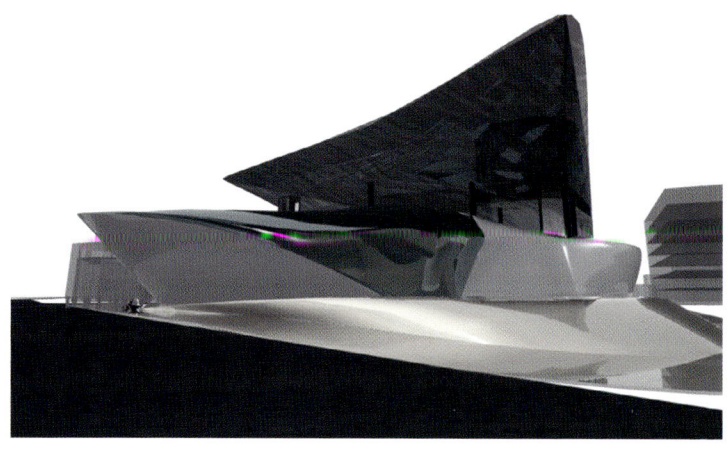

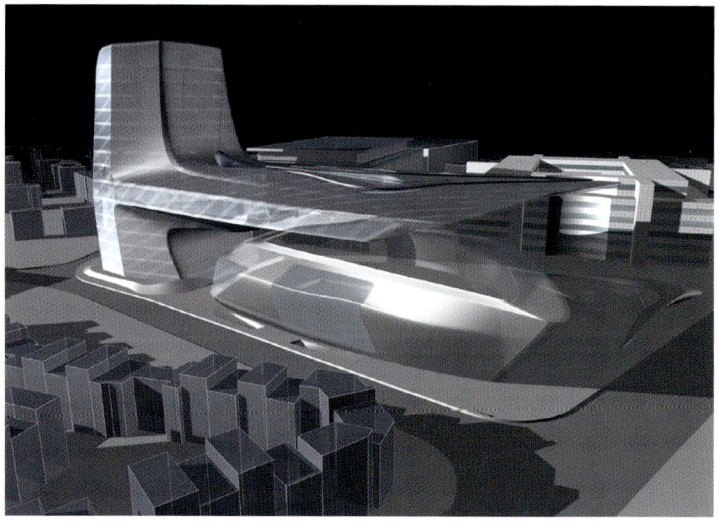

component is the larger of the two components, we think that it needs to participate in the creation of the landmark. We feel that the music centre alone could not fulfil this role against the backdrop of the massive buildings on site. Therefore, we are trying to create a monumental composition whereby the office building frames the music centre, enhancing it like a gem in its setting. The office tower projects one floor out over the volume of the music centre. This floor extends further as a large cantilevering canopy. The result is a composition that serves as a single iconic figure. The large canopy flying over the music centre stretches across the internal street to cover the stage of the outdoor performance space. This canopy also articulates a soft threshold between urban corner and campus. The concept for the music

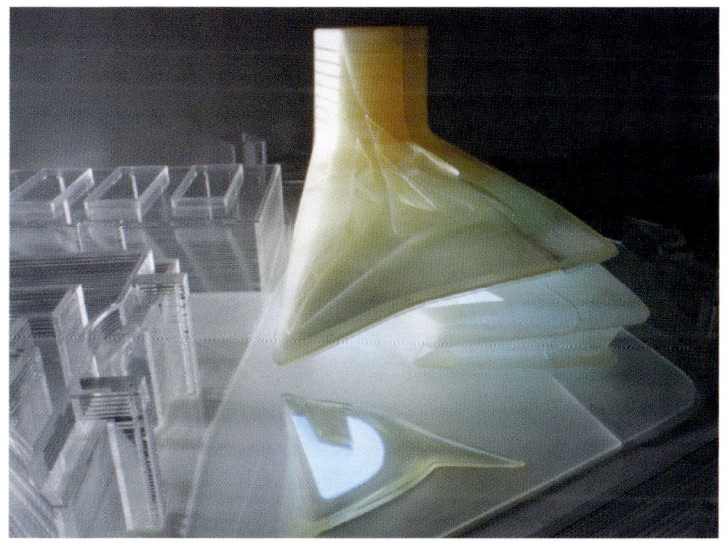

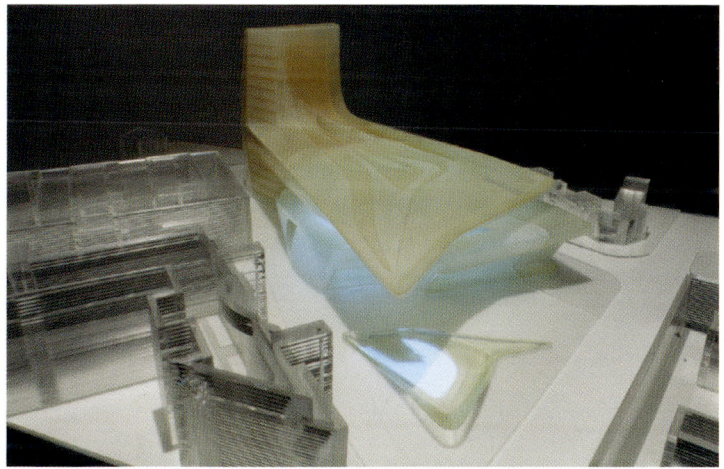

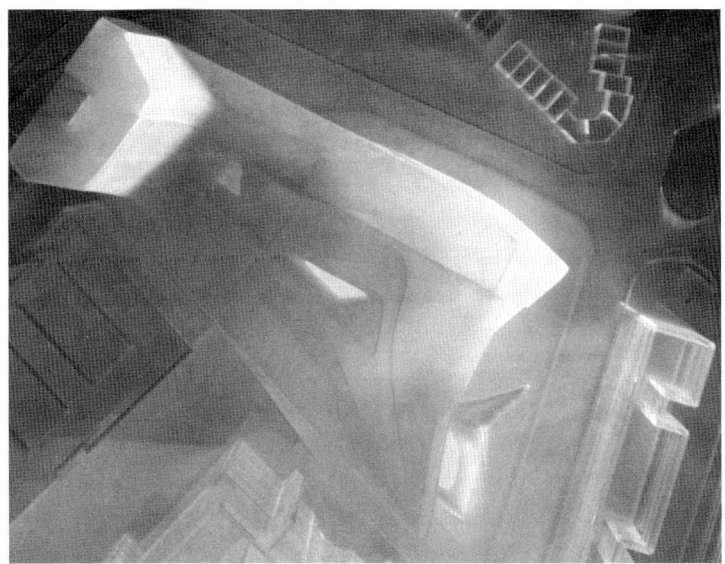

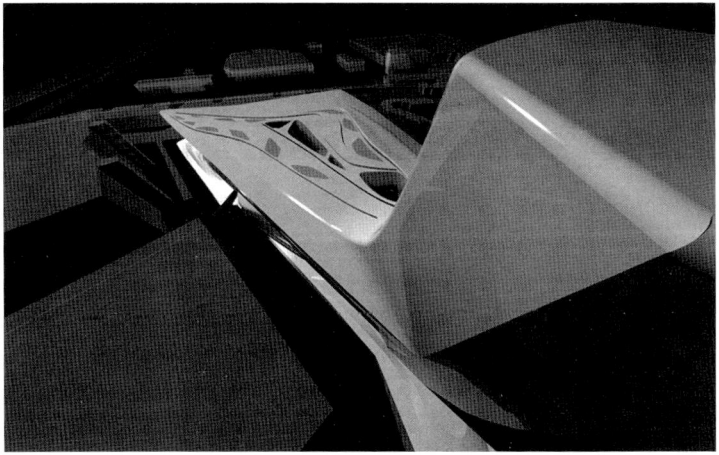

centre is the idea of nesting volumes, and an onion-like layering of skins. The overall volume of the music centre contains four volumes of similar shape but different size: Studio 1 (for the BBC Symphony Orchestra and the BBC Symphony Chorus), Studio 2 (for the BBC Concert Orchestra and the BBC Singers), the cinema and the rehearsal room. Each of these volumes in turn has an inner rectilinear volume and an outer, more curve-linear shell. The space between inner and outer shell is utilized by the belts of ancillary spaces. Deep openings cut through these shells to allow for natural light and views to penetrate the studio spaces. The arrangement of the studio spaces allows for a clear and convenient separation of the public access from the internal circulation of musicians and technicians, while maintaining an overall didactic transparency of the spatial composition. The Foyer space wraps the studio volumes and provides reception, café and exhibition. The tall lobby offers a dramatic view onto the composition of volumes. The cinema-volume projects into this space from above Studio 2. A mezzanine level stretches between the volumes, affording access to the balcony level of Studio 1. The office building is a tower with central access and service core. The footprint of the tower is 1,400 sqm. On level 5, the floorplate projects out to create a larger floorplate more than double the size. On level 6, the floorplate projects out further and bridges over the music centre. Here we are able to offer a fantastic floorplate of over 6000 sqm. The space is brightly lit by skylights and lightwells and affords views down to the urban plaza and across West London. The oblique openings allow glimpses into the studio spaces.

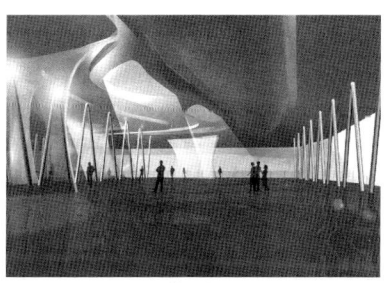

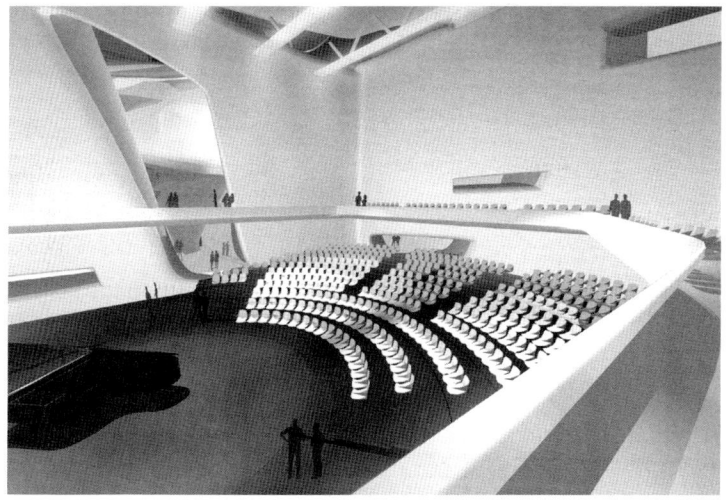

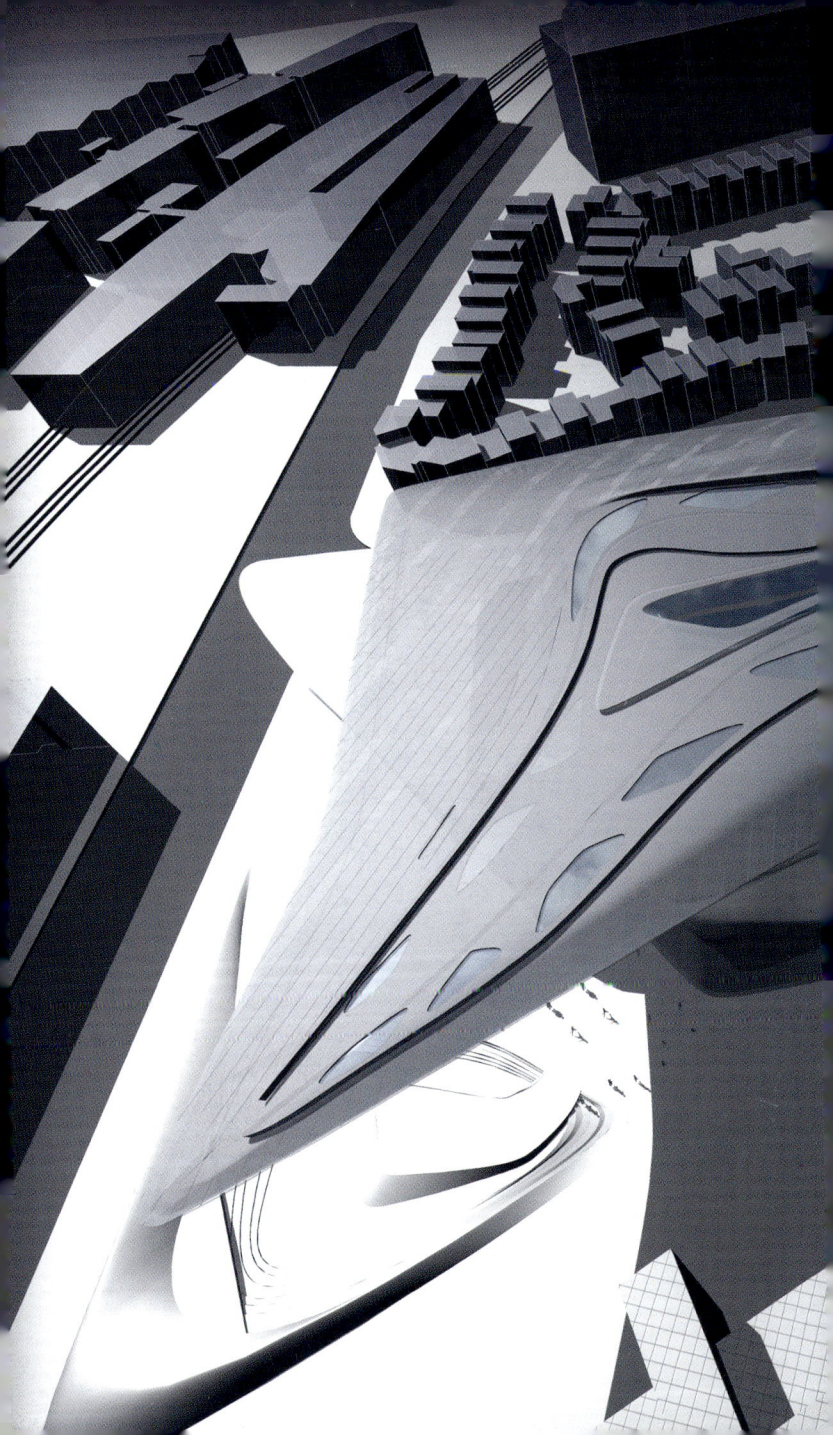

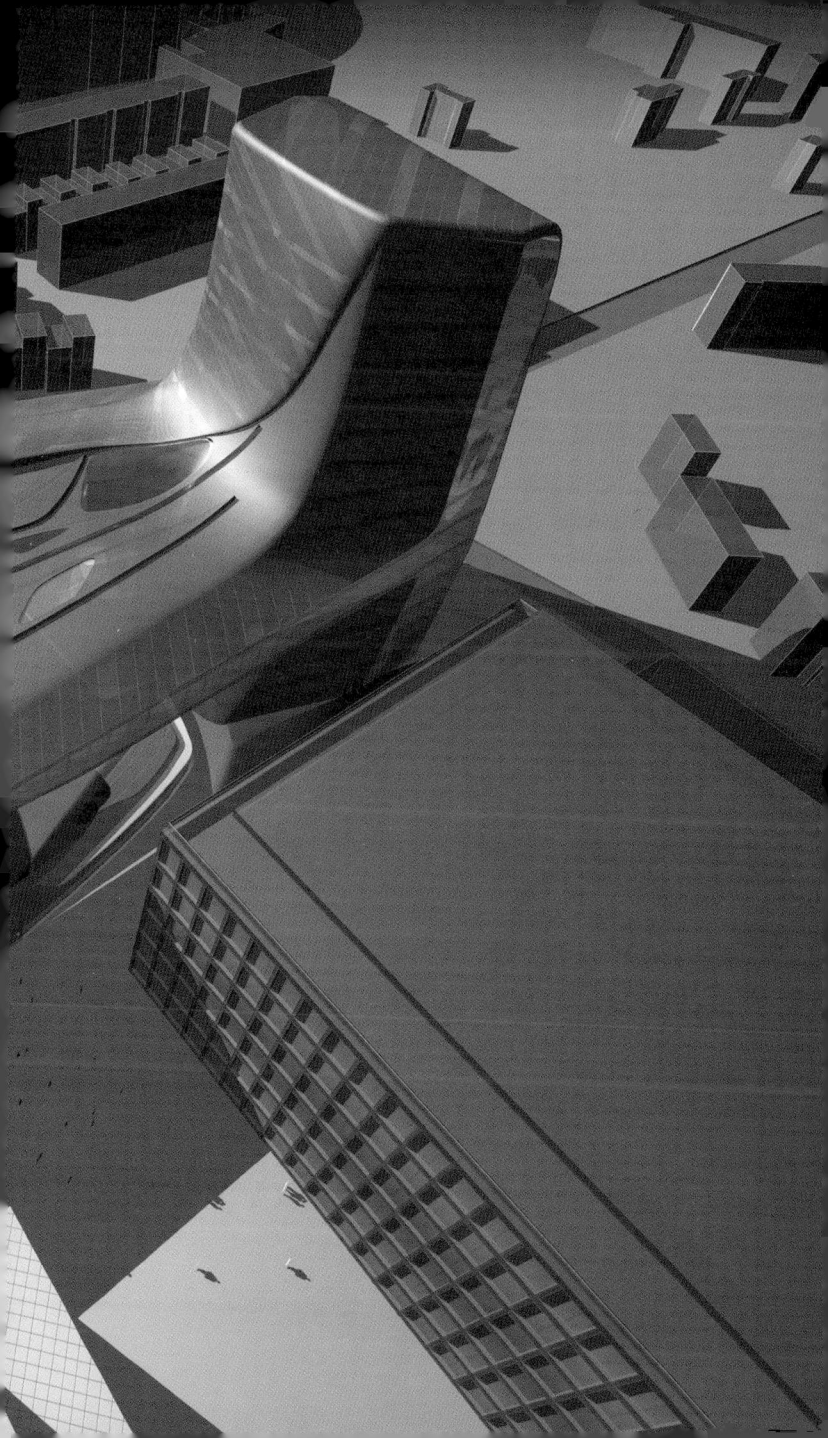

FINE ARTS CENTER, UNIVERSITY OF CONNECTICUT

The building we are proposing is a sensation that speaks to all the senses. While all the functionally dedicated spaces required by the brief are laid out and organized in a strictly functional and economic manner, we are using all the lobby and circulation spaces as a fluid mass that flows around and between the function spaces like a stream of lava. The exterior envelope follows the same curve-linear logic, suggestive of the urban, exterior flows that surround and animate the building within its context. In particular, the large performance spaces define the main body of the building by being wrapped by this fluid film or skin. The small existing theater is encircled by the fluid forms of the new building like a rock placed into a stream. In this fashion, an obstacle has been turned into an architectural event. The expressive-organic language of architecture gives this new Fine Arts Center an unmistakable character. However, this language is neither arbitrary nor idiosyncratic. Rather, it represents the fulfilment of a longstanding dream of architecture

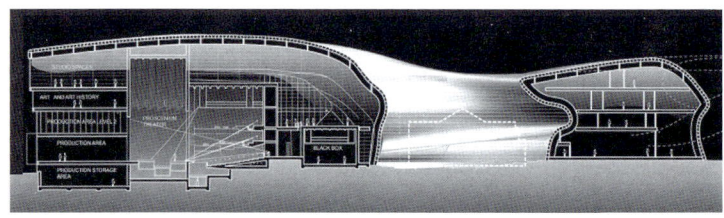

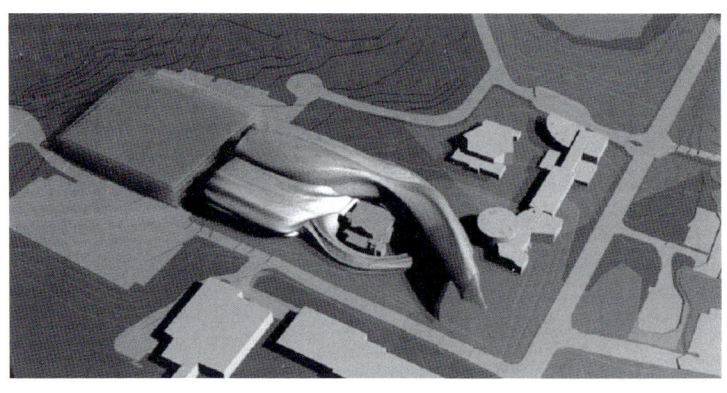

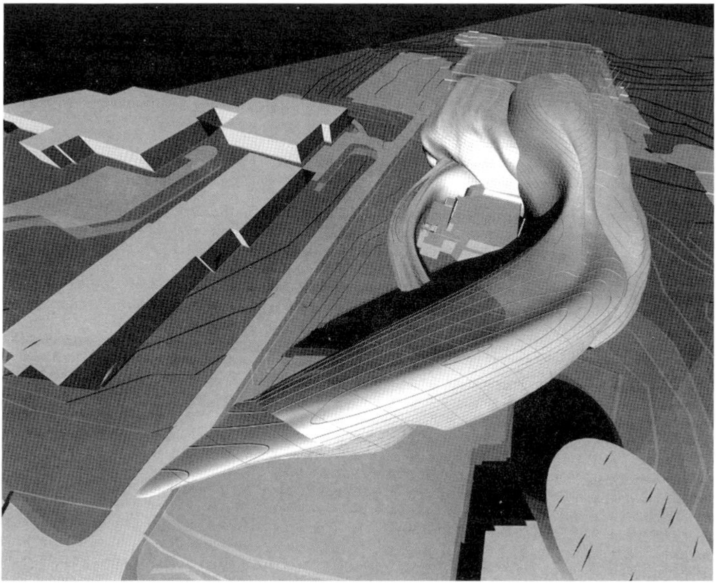

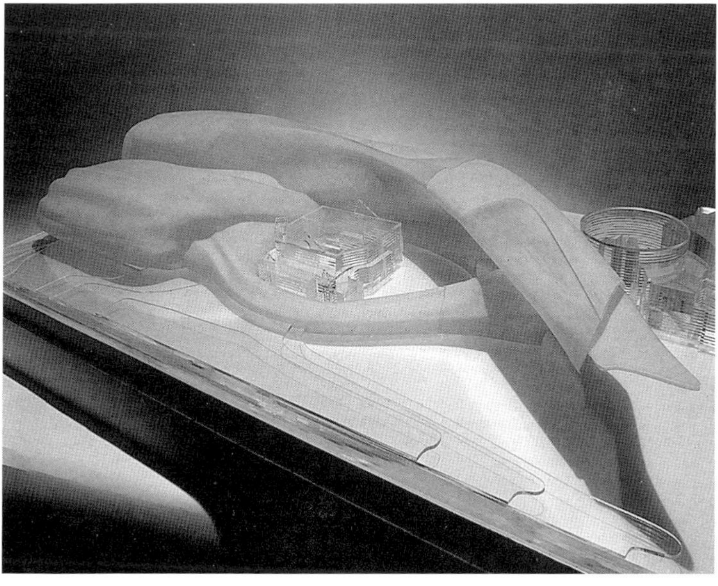

67

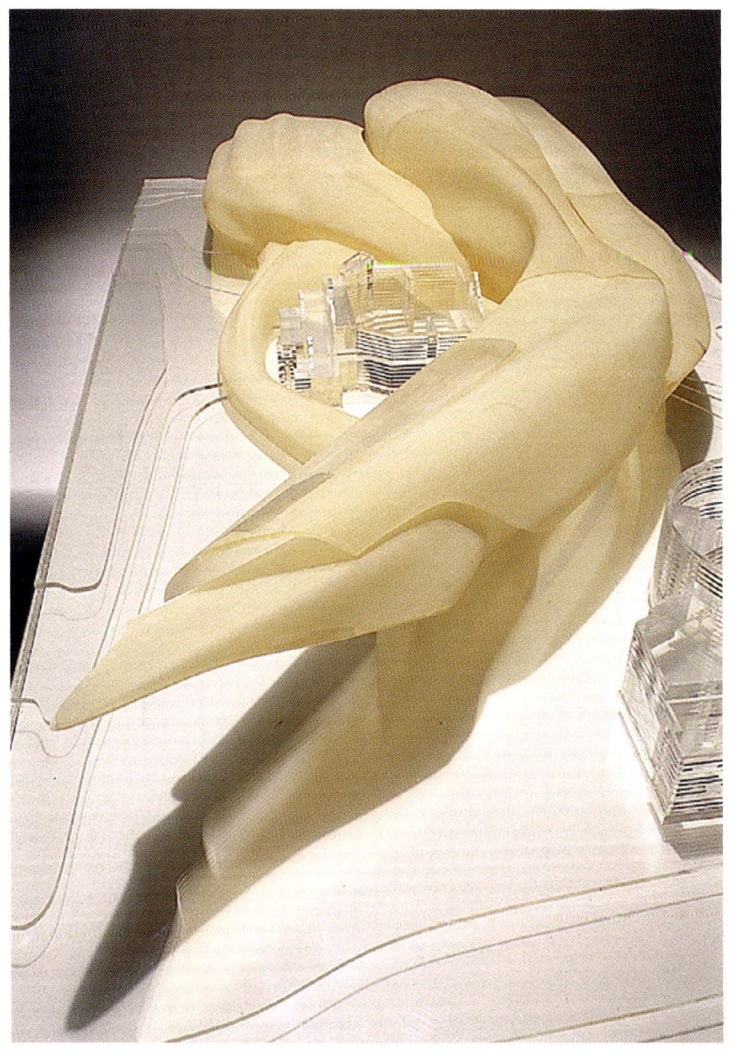

to gain the fluidity, pliancy and adaptability of natural systems. The aesthetic proposed here portends the future in as much as this new language of architecture projects the full potential of the new, state of the art, digital design and manufacturing capabilities.

FAST TRAIN STATION, FLORENCE

The key challenges of the architectural project is to create an urban event space and communication hub which is initiated by a train that is buried 25m under the ground. The task is to give expression to this hidden lifeline and to bring this underground event to the urban surface. This primary task is the point of departure for our concept: to split the ground and reveal the deep interior of the station. The slit is articulated as a tectonic fault-line along which one side lifts up while the other side bulges slightly under the pressure from below. This tectonic shift is our way of mediating the existing bank of elevated railway lines on the eastern boundary of the site with the lower urban level on the western side (ex Macelli area). Between the two

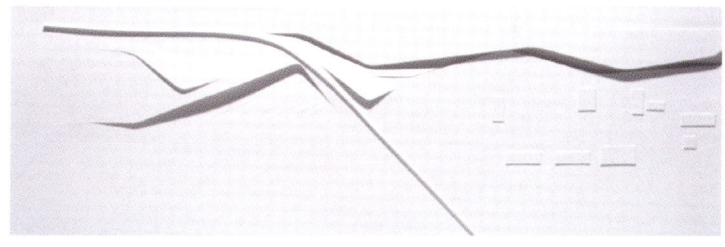

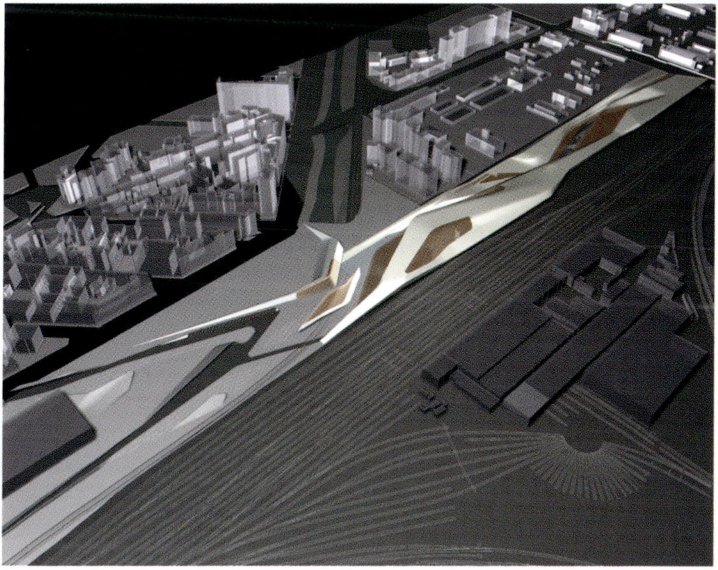

sides, a deep canyon opens up, nearly along the full length of the station, connecting the two main entrances. The play with large tectonic gestures also allows for the smooth and natural mediation of the considerable level differences between the northern and southern entrances to the site. The device of the fault-line/canyon means that all overground structures naturally lead downwards into the heart of the station, unfolding a dramatic "promenade architecturale". At the same time, the canyon offers a spectacular point of arrival for those who arrive in Florence by train. Direct glimpses of the sky are offered right as the passenger steps off the train. Also, in both directions the canyon offers an infallible means of orientation – in itself not a trivial matter in a station that measures 450 meters. The two sides of the canyon lean inwards and – at precise moments – connect. This way, no further structure is required to support this grand space.

THE DIGITAL DESIGN PROCESS (account by Maurizio Meossi)
In other words, it is possible to describe the entire creative process of the project, describing the evolution of the digital model and the techniques used for its realization. Differently to what happened in other projects developed by the office in the same period, the digital model had, in fact, its own development in the formal definition of the Station, almost autonomously from its programmatic definition; therefore the digital model has not been merely a three-dimensional tool to verify "bi-dimensional" intuitions, but it has been the main instrument of formal exploration. This relative independence made it possible to enact a dialectical relationship of continuous input and output between the digital model on one side and plans-sections (bi-dimensional drawings, the "traditional" media of architectural representation) on the other. This reciprocal interaction has gone on the layout of the final drawings, allowing the formal research to be pushed until the very last minute. From a strictly technical point of view, the modeling has been an application of the "cross-sections/surface" technique, a method that (through the subsequent application of two 3ds Max commands) allows the definition of a complex surface (mesh) starting with at least two curves (splines) that characterize its main geometry. The software generates the surface through a process of interpolation, leaving the geometrical control on the starting curves, whose vertices become sort of "grips"

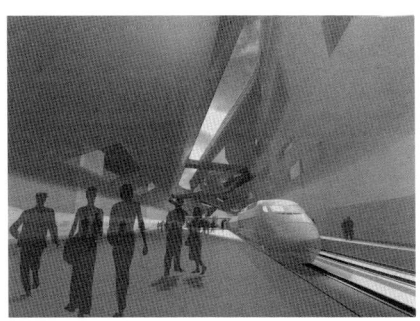

through which it is possible to "sculpt" and "shape" the resulting surface. This peculiar property of the solid modeling tools of the new generation (3ds Max as well as Maya or Rhyno) is due to two basic features: first, they operate in a parametric way, meaning that it is possible to control each single operation through numeric values (corresponding for example to coordinates of points, movements in space, or height of extrusion of a shape, or function degree used by the geometric interpolation algorithm, etc.), that are constantly modifiable; second, the software maintains a "historical memory" of the operations made on each single object, so that it is possible to go back and modify the "primitive" geometrical entity (in our case the generative curves) at each moment of the process. Trying to resume the key steps of the entire process we have:

1- starting curves definition, in this case, horizontal slices of the "canyon", traced on the basis of a preliminary study with physical models; the sequential application of the commands "cross-sections" and "surface" generates the complex surface that represents the first digital study model;

2- digital manipulation of the obtained surface: acting on the vertices of the generative curves, it is possible to accurately control the overall geometry, emphasizing the formal aspect of the research;

3- cross sections (in our case at least 10) are extracted from the digital model; the sections become the basis for the structural and programmatic development, with consequent modifications in the horizontal sections (that we can now start to call "proto-plans");

4- an updated model is built according to the new horizontal sections, starting a reiterative process of points 2 to 4, in order to obtain simultaneously functional optimization and satisfying formal results.

Experimentation on the digital model has been of great importance also for the "materic" study of the Station wrapping: passages from opaque to transparent surfaces are made using "carving" operations on the same complex surface; a change of material does not mean geometrical discontinuity. From representation technique to active designing tool, able to modify the way we conceive the architectural project: this is the main step represented by digital modeling.

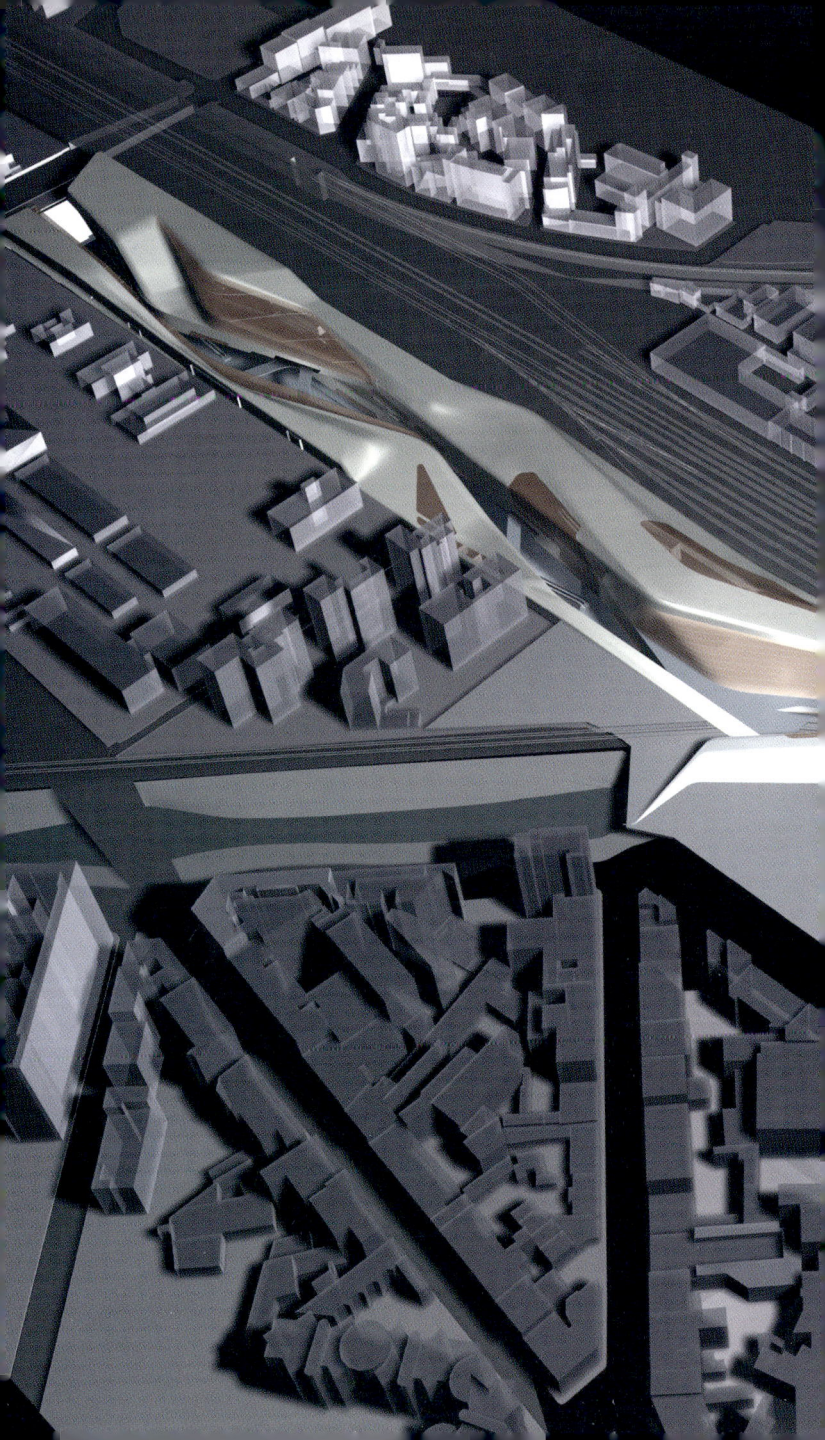

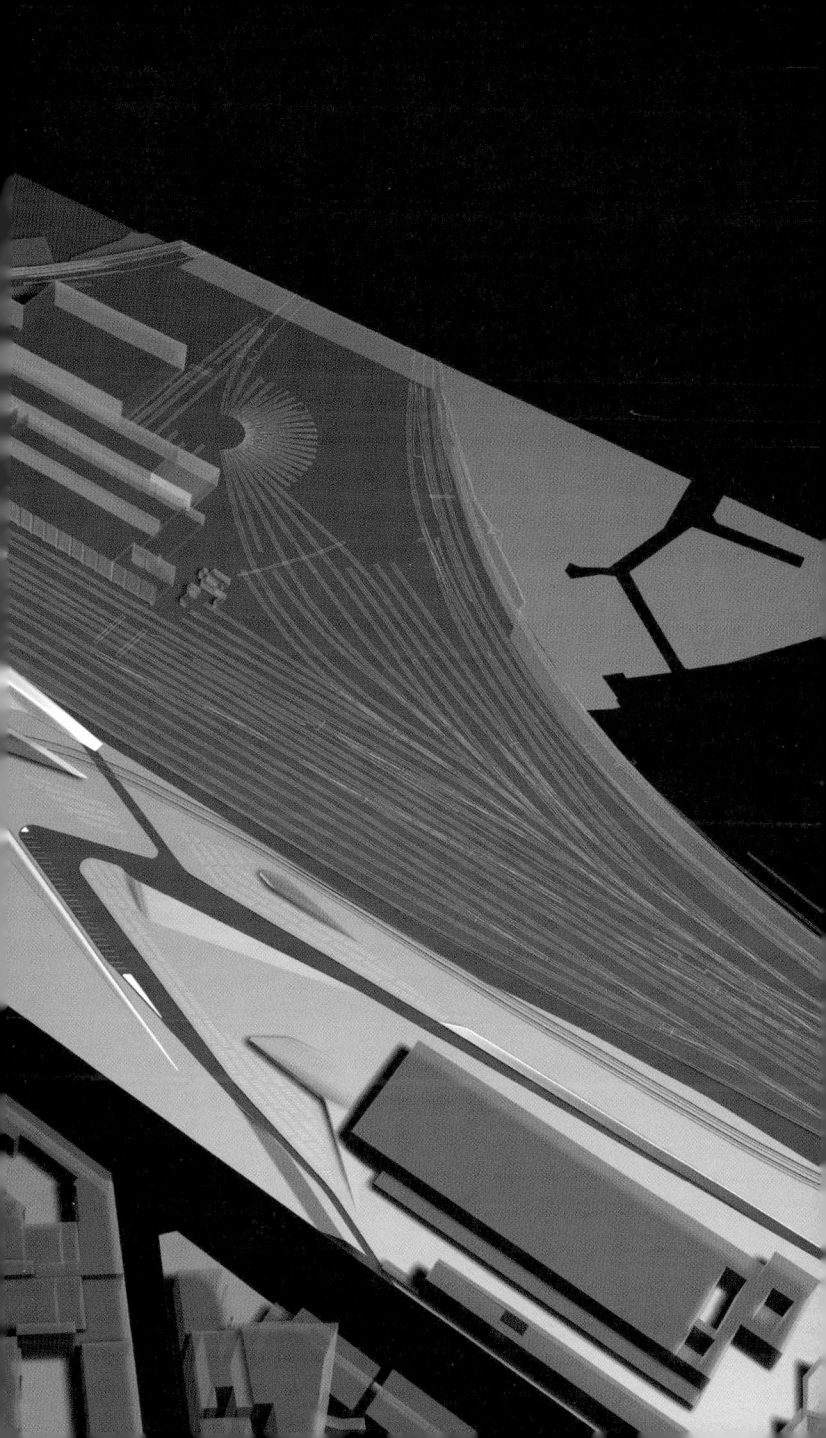

FAST TRAIN STATION, NAPLES

The key challenge of the architectural project is to create a well-organized transport interchange that can simultaneously serve as a new landmark that announces the approach to Naples – a new gateway to the city. This is the first reason why we chose to conceive the new station as a bridge above the tracks. The task is to give expression to the imposition of a new through-station that can also act as the nucleus of a new business park that will link the various surrounding towns. This is the second reason why we conceived the station as a bridge that provides an urbanized public link across the tracks. In fact, the station is to be approached from two sides. There is no justification in privileging one of these two sides. Therefore, the station might have two

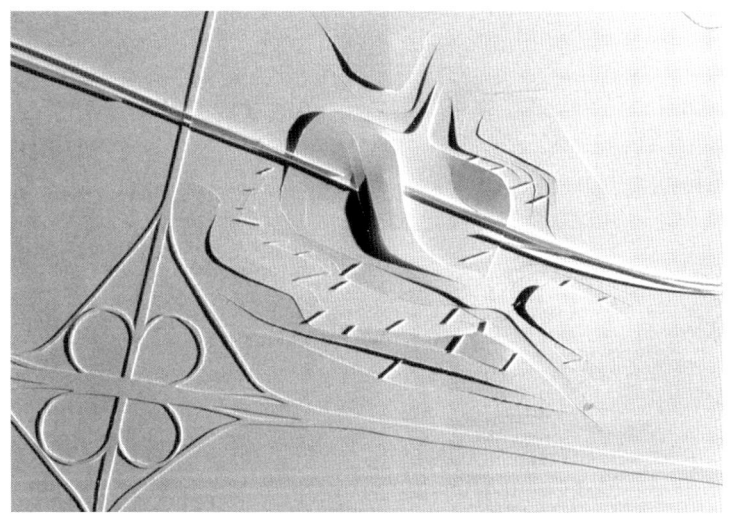

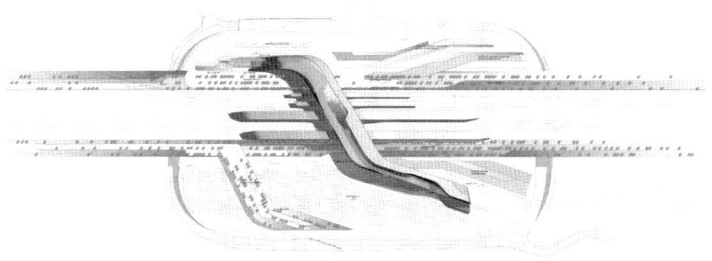

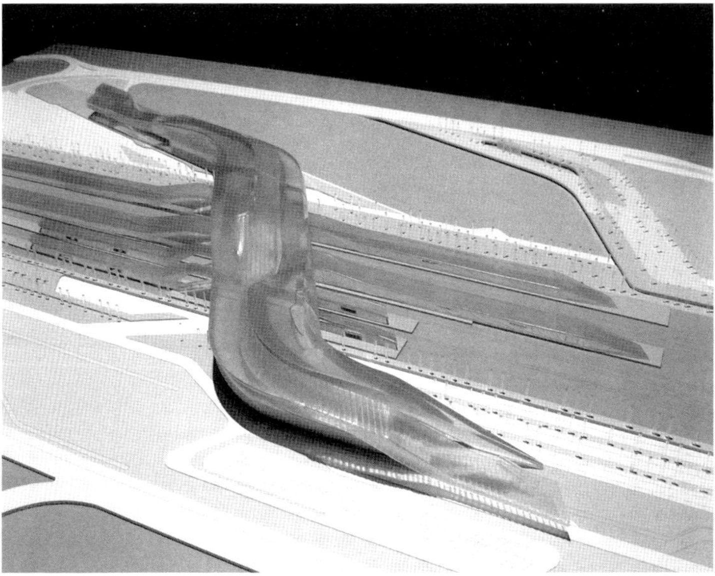

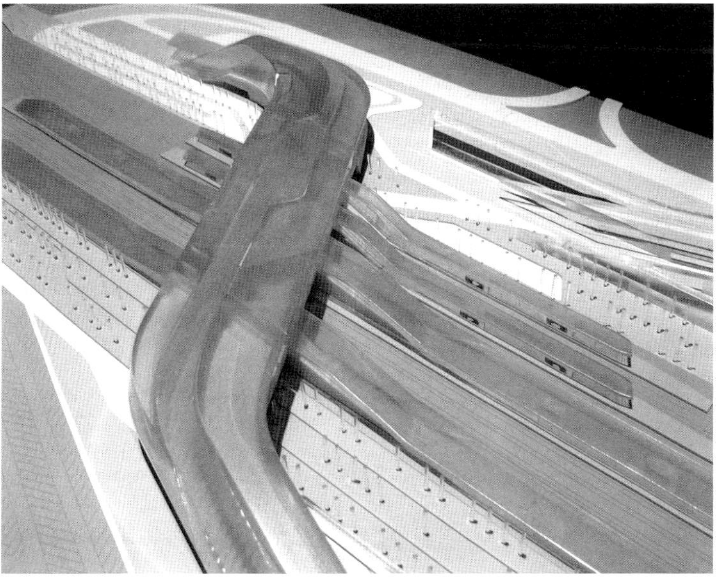

75

entrances – one on either side of the tracks. By implication, the central functions and the main visible body of the station should ideally be placed in the center above the tracks, thus equally addressing both sides. This is the third and perhaps most compelling reason why we think that the station should be designed as a bridge. The architectural language proposed is geared towards the articulation of movement and allows for the smooth integration of all the flows and traffic lines that intersect in this new transport interchange. It ties in naturally with the bundle of railway lines and access roads which characterize this artificial terrain. This open and dynamic quality of the architectural figure is pursued further within the interior of the building, where the trajectories of the travellers determine the geometry of the space. The facilitation of obvious and easy access, as well as the smooth guidance of all movements within, is the fundamental ethos of our design.

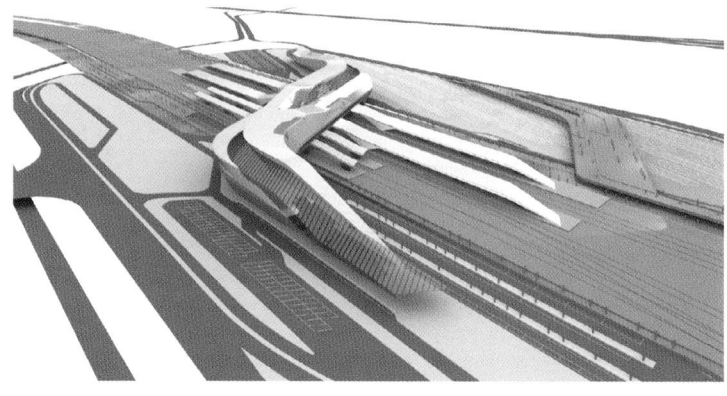

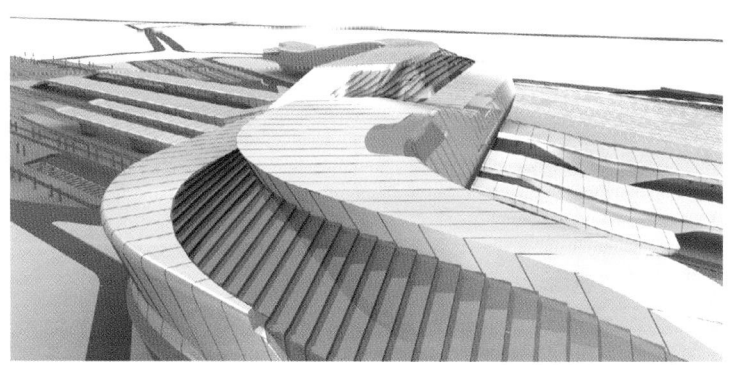

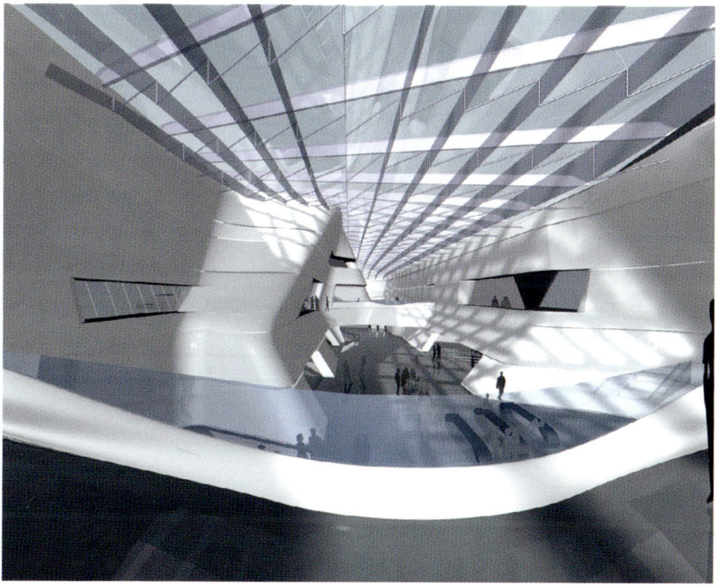

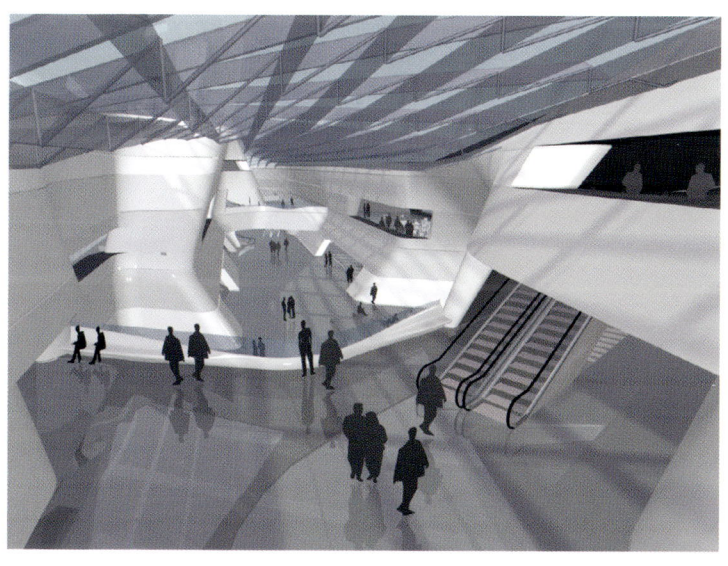

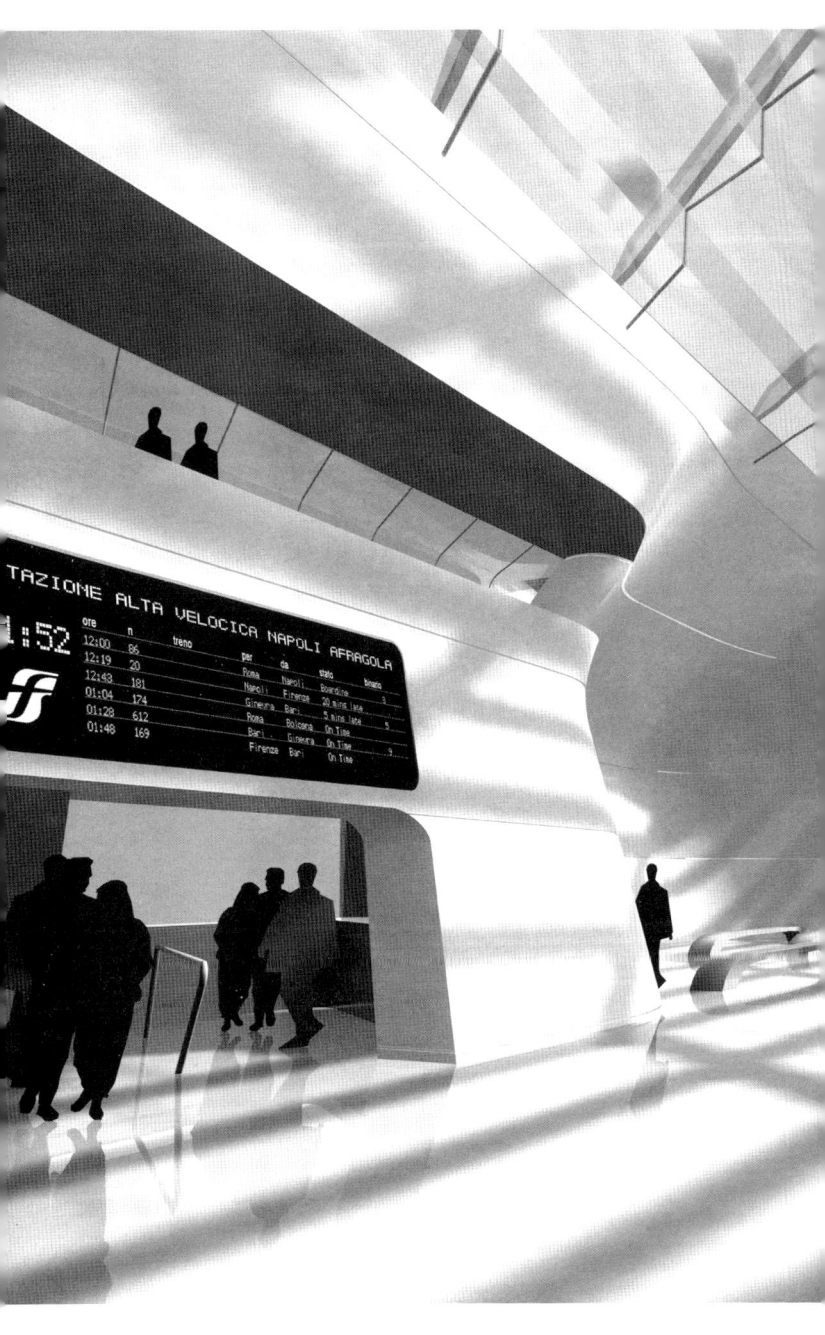

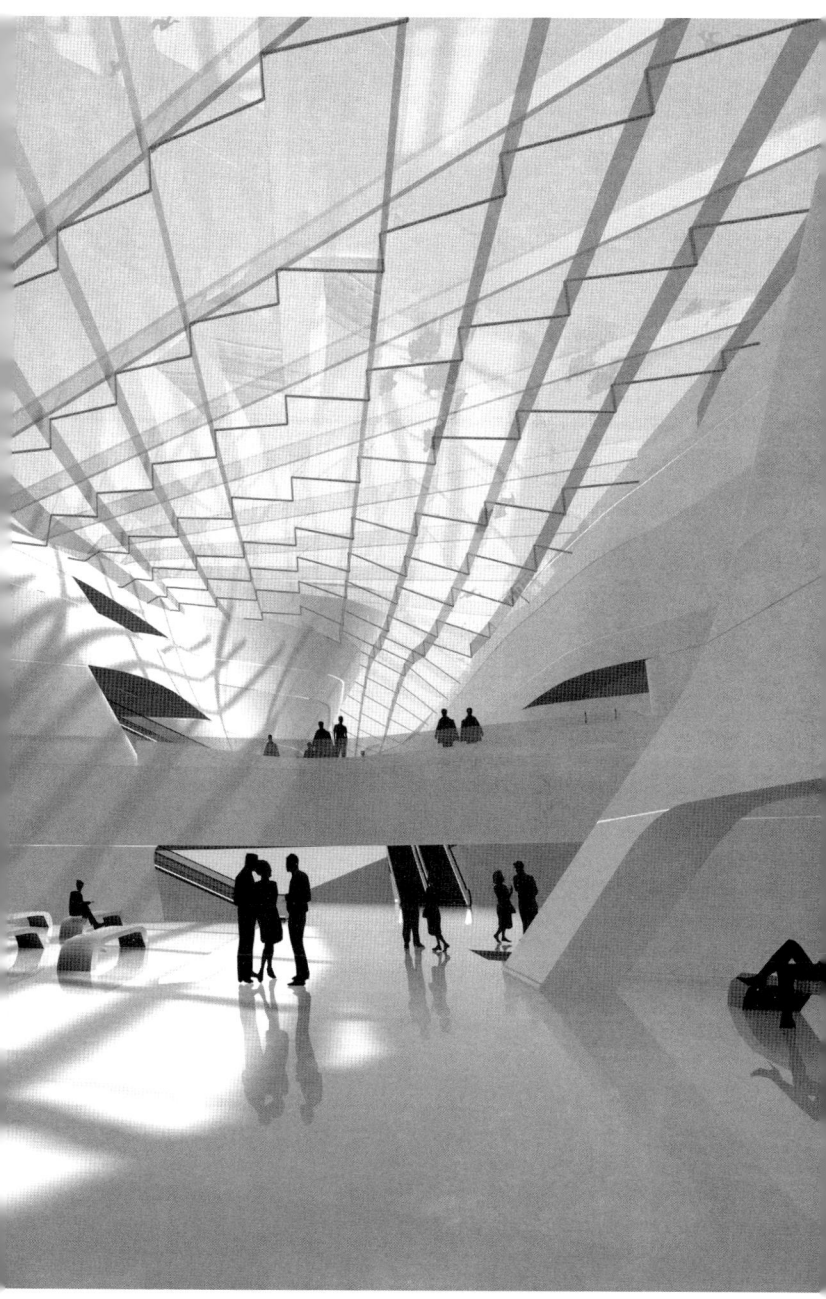

80

THE TEMPORARY GUGGENHEIM, TOKYO

Odasiba Island seems a perfect place to establish a site of cultural experimentation. Here, a very dynamic urban space emerges, built upon synthetic land and animated by the entrepreneurial spirit of rapid development. In this

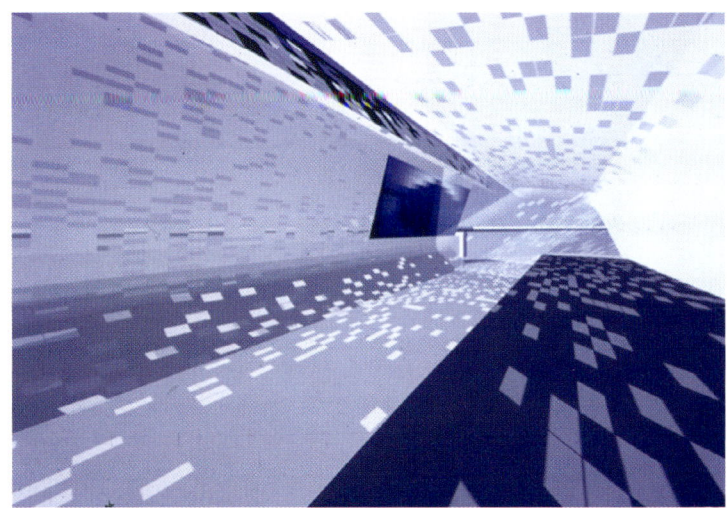

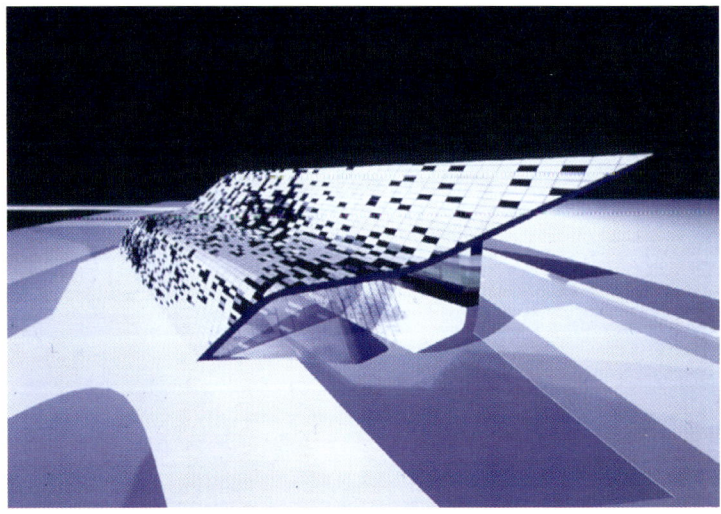

context, the 10-year intervention of the temporary Guggenheim will be an instant cultural hot spot and a catalyst for related activities. With respect to the architectural iconography, the structure should signify the creative employment of state-of-the-art science and technology. As a visitor experience, the object has to excite curiosity and desire. A considerable degree of strangeness is indispensable. The project – like any true object of desire – will

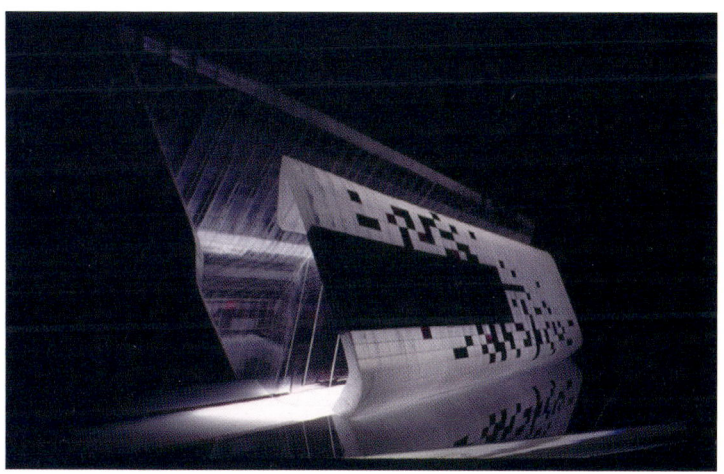

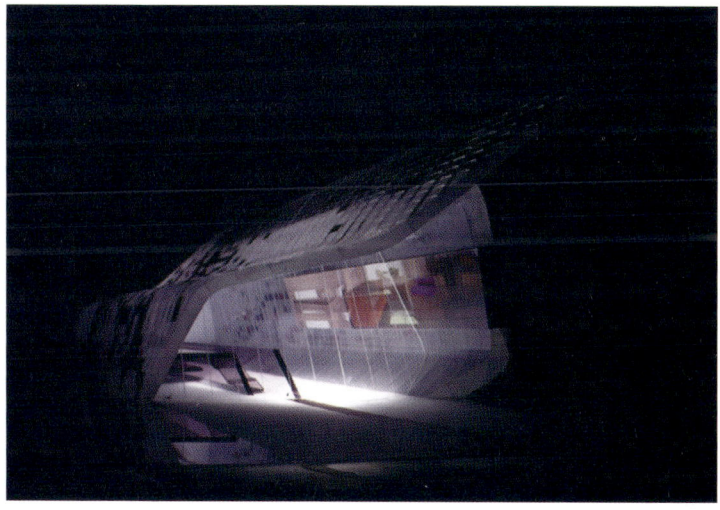

at first appear mysterious, an unknown territory waiting to be discovered and explored. In line with the temporary nature of the structure, we are opting for a lightweight envelope. A strong signature figure is created as two folded planes – like sheets of paper – lean against each other and encapsulate a generous space. This image of an elegant lightweight wrapping seems an appropriate response, since a space for changing exhibitions needs to be receptive to constant internal redefinition. However, the empty space itself is already its own attraction. Although the spatial concept is extremely simple – in effect the parallel extrusion of three simple sections – the size, level of abstraction and dynamic profile of the folded planes ensure an exhilarating spatial sensation. The diagonal cleft at the top exerts a dramatic sense of vertigo as the light washes down the tilted plane. At both ends, the three extrusions are cut off at different angles. This simple move effectively articulates the ends and allows us to emphasize the entrance zone with a dramatic gesture. A further aspect to be noted is the quality of the skin. We are proposing a snakeskin-like pixelation that allows the formally-coherent integration of various surface performances. The primary cladding material would be large-scale ceramic tiles (offering smooth surfaces and brilliant colors). These would be interspersed by light-boxes which allow further daylight to penetrate the space, as well as acting as an artificial light source at night. Further panels would be photovoltaic elements. Finally, we are proposing to embed a large media screen – in the form of honeycomb-based "smart slabs". The media screen would be nearly camouflaged into the overall animation of the skin. Internally, the skin operates according to the same concept but is aesthetically much more muted. Here light, ventilation and heating are incorporated within the pixel logic.

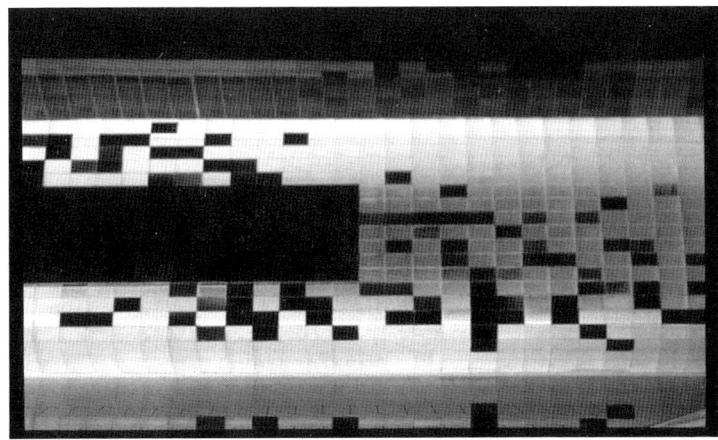

GUGGENHEIM MUSEUM, TAICHUNG

The design proposal is based on the concept of the museum as an ever-changing event space. To emphasize the aspect of transformability of the space, we would like to explore the possibility of equipping the new museum with something like a "stage-machinery". We devised a series of large-scale kinetic elements that offer the option of radically transforming the

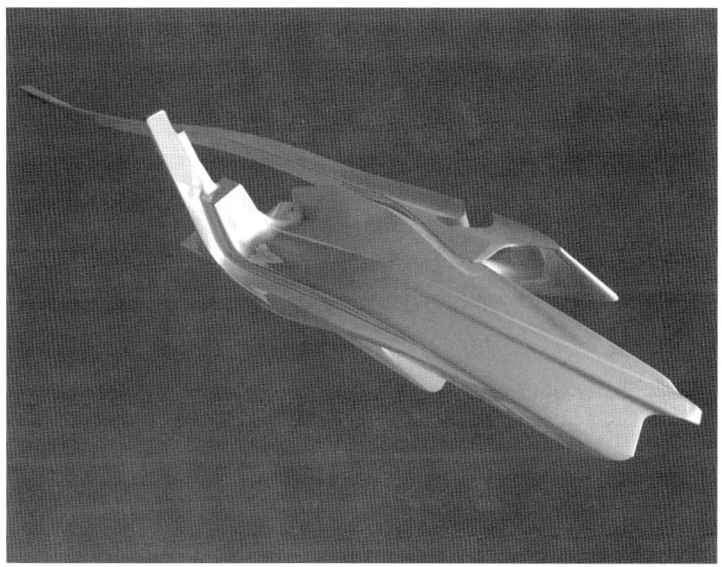

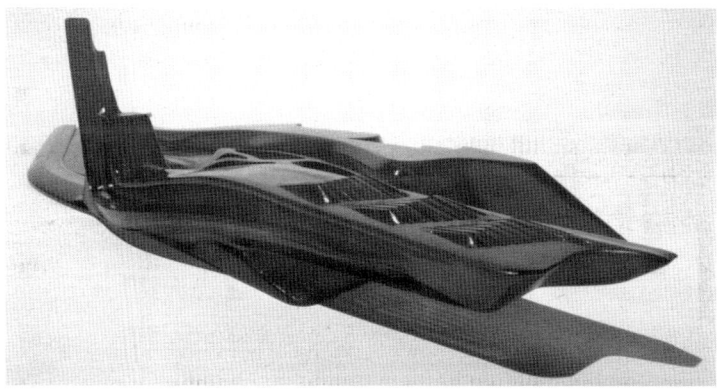

arrangement of the gallery spaces. We would also like to make this dramatic transformation of the space itself a spectacle, visible even on the outside appearance of the building. Thus, the internal reconfiguration of the exhibition spaces creates a public sensation within the urban scenery. The site is tied into a masterplan of two crossing axes that give an organizing structure

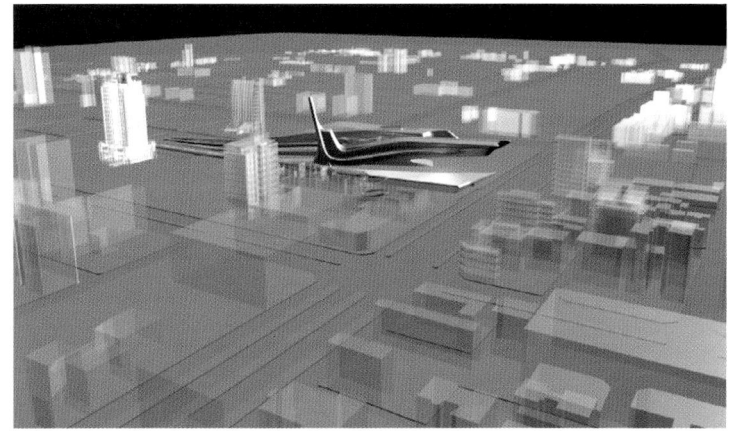

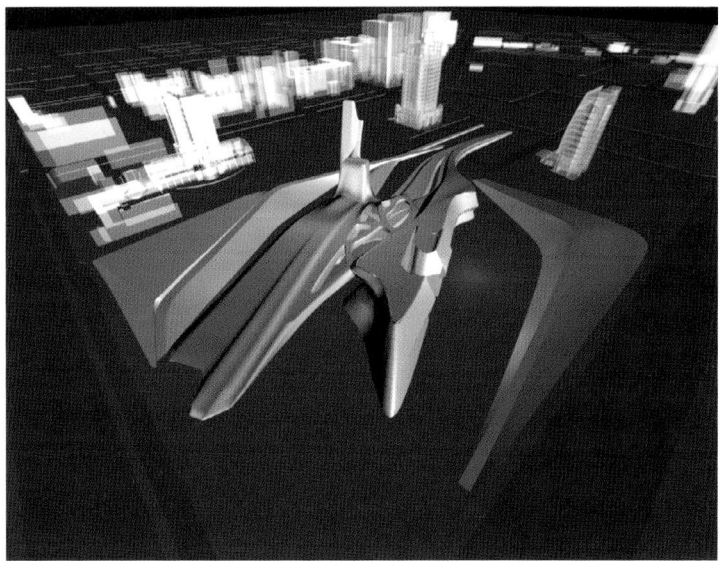

to the ensemble of four new landmark buildings that will comprise the Guggenheim Museum, the new town hall, the city assembly and the national opera. This arrangement implies that the museum will be approached from two main sides. This double orientation leads to the idea of a large lobby space that can be approached from two opposing ends and thus cuts

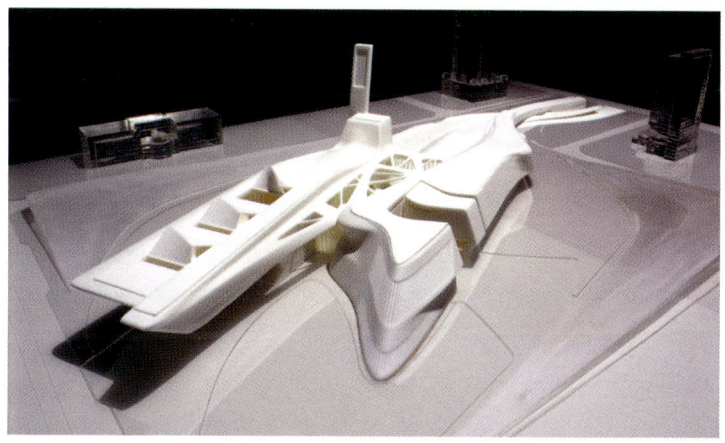

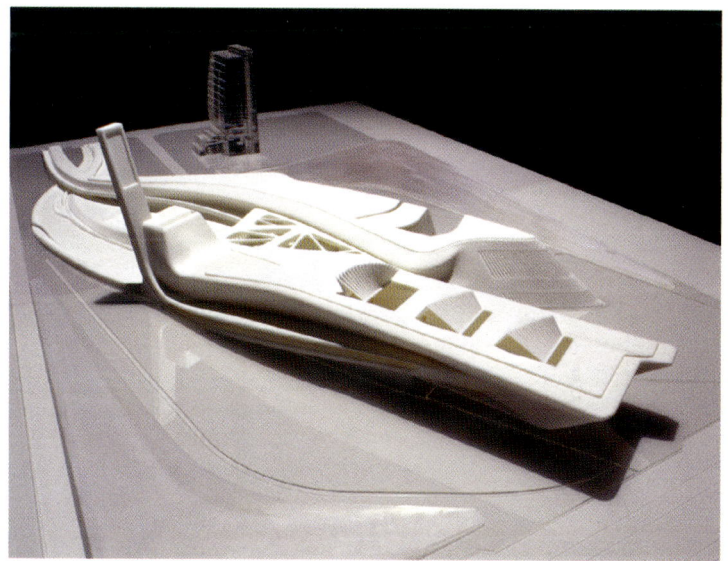

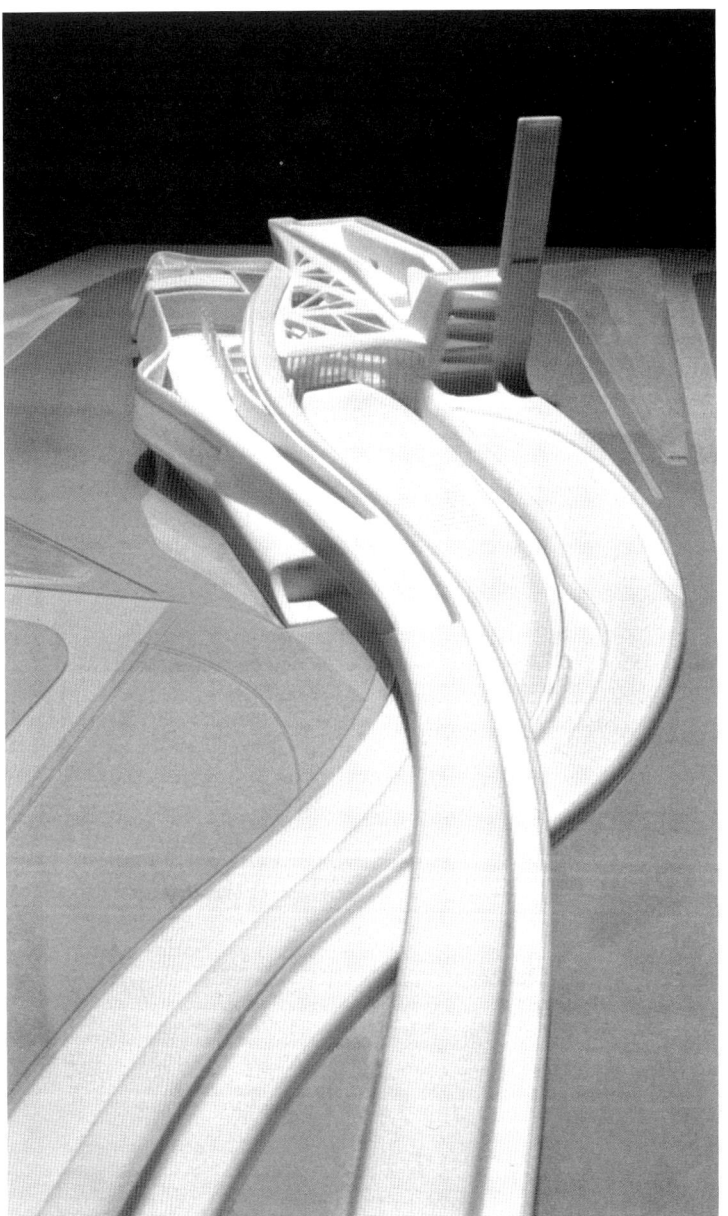

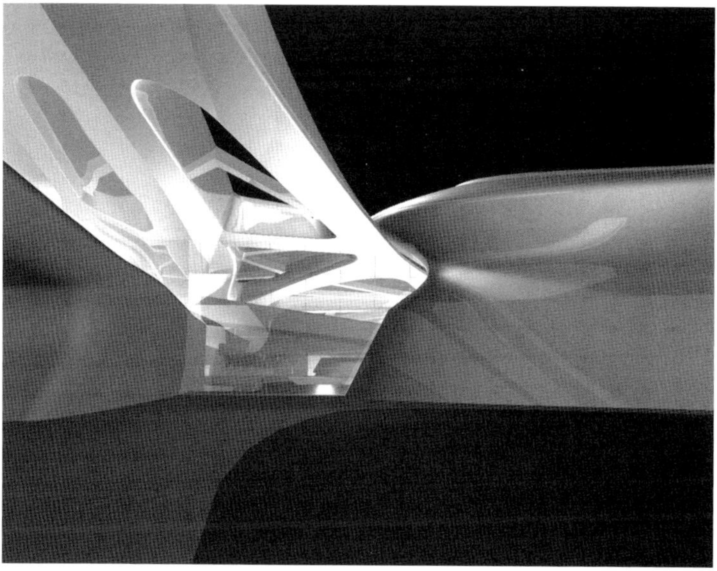

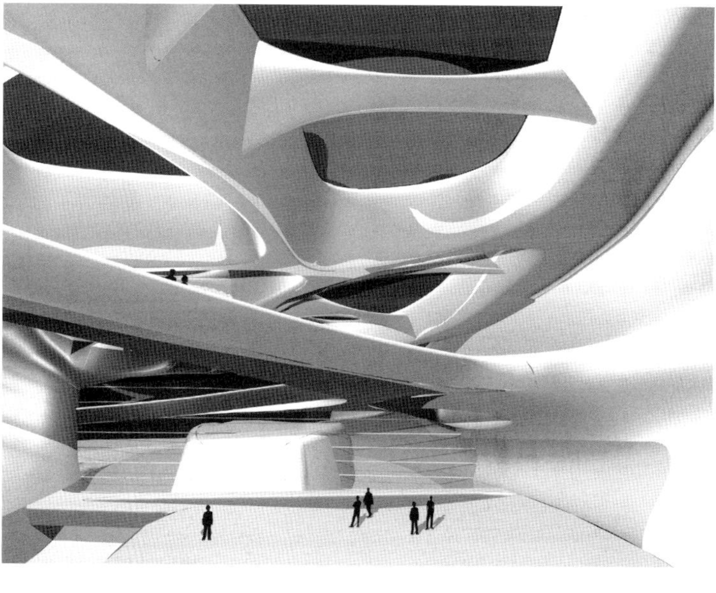

a public path through the museum. Much of the internal organization of the museum follows from this initial move, motivated by the urban configuration. The building gradually emerges from a soft landscape formation. The formal language and architectural articulation is premised on the idea that the building bleeds into the open public space of the urban axis. The overall dynamism and fluidity of the elongated form suggests an emphasis of movement through and around the building. Both the public flow through the building as well as the internal circulation through the exhibition spaces is expressed by means of swooping ramps. Although the building can be approached from both ends, these two ends are articulated rather differently. On Taichungkang Road, the building offers its urban edge with a severe cantilevering volume which projects towards the Taichungkang Road like a huge canopy. The opposing end facing the future park-scape of the new urban ensemble is characterized by curved ramps merging into the building.

Further Reading

Mitchell 1990 – William J. Mitchell, Design Worlds, The MIT Press, Cambridge, Mass. 1990, chapter 3, "The Logic of Architecture".
Foucault 1970 – Michel Foucault, *The Order of Things*, Tavistock Publications, London 1970, chapters 2, 5.
Foucault 2002 – Michel Foucault, *The Archaeology of Knowledge*, Routledge, New York 2002.
Benedict 1992 – Michael Benedict, *Cyberspace*, New York 1992.
Rowe, Slutzky 1976 – Colin Rowe, Robert Slutzky, "Transparency: Literal and Phenomenal", in *The Mathematics of the Ideal Villa and Other Essays*, The MIT Press Cambridge, Mass. 1976.
Kipnis 1997 – Jeffrey Kipnis, "P-Tr's Progress", in El Croquis 83, 1997, special issue *Peter Eisenman 1990-1997*.
Holtzman 1994 – Steven R. Holtzman, *Digital Mantras - The Languages of Abstract and Virtual Worlds*, The MIT Press, Cambridge, Mass. 1994, chapter 6, "Postwar Serialism", chapter 7, "Chomsky", chapter 8, "Coda".
Massumi 1998 – Brian Massumi, "Sensing the Virtual, Building the Insensible", in *AD*, special issue *Hypersurface Architecture*, London 1998.
Rajchman 1997 – John Rajchman, "The Virtual House", in *ANY Magazine*, no. 19-20, 1997.
Frazer 1995 – John Frazer, "Introduction" to *An Evolutionary Architecture*, Architectural Association, London 1995.
Croquis 103 – *El Croquis*, no. 103, special issue *Zaha Hadid 1996-2001 - Landscape as a Plan*.
Schumacher 2002 – Patrik Schumacher, *The Autopiesis of Architecture*, in Zaha Hadid, Patrik Scumacher (eds.), *Latent Utopias - Experiments within Contemporary Architecture*, Springer Verlag, Wien-New York 2002.
Schumacher 2003 – Patrik Schumacher, *Mechanisms of Radical Innovation*, in Peter Noever (ed.), *Zaha Hadid Architektur*, catalog of the exhibition, Museum of Applied Arts, Hatje Canz Verlag, Wien 2003.

Project Credits

CENTER FOR CONTEMPORARY ART, ROME

Client : Italian Ministry of Culture & Ministry of Public Works.
Design: Zaha Hadid with Patrik Schumacher.
Project architect: Gianluca Racana.
Production team: Ana M.Cajao, Fabio Ceci, Matteo Grimaldi, Paolo Matteuzzi, Mario Mattia, Maurizio Meossi, Luca Peralta, Barbara Pfenningstorff, Gianluca Ruggeri , Luca Segarelli, Anja Simons, Maria Velceva, Paolo Zilli.
Design Team: Gianluca Racana, Dillon Lin, Christos Passas, Oliver Domeisen, Shumon Bazar, Ali Mangera, Barbara Pfenningstorff, Ana M.Cajao, Sonia Villaseca, Jee-Eun Lee, James Lim, Sara Klomps, Bergendy Cooke, Jorge Ortega', Woody Yao, Graham Modlen, Markus Dochantschi, Ana Sotrel, Heverin, Hemendra Kothari, Zahira El Nazel.
Associated Architect: ABT, David Sabatello, Piercarlo Rampini, Paolo Olivi, Marco Valerio Faggiani, Paolo Bisogni.
Structure: Anthony Hunt Associates - Les Postawa, Dave Weale; OK Design Group - Simone Di Cintio, Marco Barone.
M&E: Max Fordham and Partners - Henry Luker, Neil Smith; OK Design Group - Carlo Rossi, Pete Fanelli, Domenico Raponi.
Lighting: Equation Lighting - Mark Hensman, Paolo Giovane.
Acoustics: Paul Gilleron Acoustics - Paul Gilleron.

ART CENTER, GRAZ – COMPETITION

Design: Zaha Hadid with Patrik Schumacher.
Project team: Gianluca Racana, David Gerber, Sonia Villaseca, Paola Catterin.

QUEBEC NATIONAL LIBRARY, MONTREAL

Design: Zaha Hadid with Patrik Schumacher.
Project team: Stephane Hof, Dillon Lin, Lida Charsouli, Sonia Villaseca, Chris Dopheide, Djordje Stojanovic, Garin O'Aivazian.

ONE NORTH MASTERPLAN, SINGAPORE

Client: JVC, Singapore.
Design: Zaha Hadid with Patrik Schumacher.
Project architects: David Gerber, Dillon Lin, Gunther Koppelhuber, Markus Dochantschi.
Project team: Silvia Forlati, Kim Thornton, Rodrigo O'Malley, David Mah, Yael Brosilovski, Hon Kong Chee, Fernando Perez Vera.
Urban strategy: Lawrence Barth.
Competition team: David Gerber, Edgar Gonzalez, Chris Dopheide, David Salazar, Tiago Correia, Ken Bostock, Paola Cattarin, Dillon Lin, Barbara Kuit, Woody K.T. Yao.
Infrastructural engineers: Arup: Simon Hancock, Ian Carradice, David Johnston.
Transport engineers: MVA: Paul Williams, Tim Booth

Landscape architects: Cicada Private Limited.
Lighting planners: LPA: Karou Mende.
Planning tool: B consultants: Tom Barker, Graeme Jennings.

BMW Central Building, Leipzig

Client: BMW.
Design: Zaha Hadid with Patrik Schumacher.
Project architects: Jim Heverin, Lars Teichmann.
Project team: Matthias Frei, Jan Huebener, Annette Bresinsky, Manuela Gatto, Fabian Hecker, Cornelius Schlotthauer, Wolfgang Sunder, Anneka Wegener, Markus Planteu, Robert Neumayr.
Competition team: Lars Teichmann, Stephane Hof, Eva Pfannes, Manuela Gatto, Tina Gegoric, Cesare Griffa, Filippo Innocenti, Maurizio Meossi, Debora Laub, Zetta Kotsioni, Yasha Grobmann, Liam Young, Niki Neerpasch, Keneth Bostok, Djordje Stojanovic, Leyre Villoria, Christiane Fashek, Eric Tong.
Landscape architects: Gross. Max (Edinburgh, UK).
Structural engineer: Anthony Hunts Assoc., (London, UK).
Cost: IFB Dr. Braschel AG, (Berlin, Germany).
Light design: Equation Lighting, London.

Ice-storm, Lounging Environment

Client: Museum for Applied Arts, Vienna.
Design: Zaha Hadid & Patrik Schumacher.
Project architects: Thomas Vietzke, Woody Yao.

Z-Scape, Lounging Furniture

Manufacturer: Sawaya-Moroni, Milan.
Project architects: Carolin Voet, Patrik Schumacher.

Fine Arts Center, University of Connecticut

Client: University of Connecticut
Design: Zaha Hadid with Patrick Schumacher.
Competition team: Juan I. Aranguren, Simon Kim, Karim Muallem, Elena Perez Guembe, Theodore Spyropoulos.
Structure: Bob Lang, Ove Arup.
Services: Nigel Tonks, Ove Arup.
Acoustics: Richard Cowell, Ove Arup.
Theater projects: David Staples.
Cost consultant: Sam Mackenzie, Davis Langdon & Everest..

BBC Music Centre, London

Client: BBC.
Design: Zaha Hadid & Patrik Schumacher.

Project team: Steven Hatzellis, Graham Modlen, Ergian Alberg, Karim Muellem, Ram Ahronov, Adriano De Gioannis, Simon Kim, Yansong Ma.
Structure: Bob Lang, Ove Arup.
Services: Nigel Tonks, Ove Arup.
Acoustics: Richard Cowell, Ove Arup.
Theater consultant: Anne Minors.
Cost consultant: Sam Mackenzie, Davis Langdon & Everest.

NEW FAST TRAIN STATION, FLORENCE

Client: TAV.
Design: Zaha Hadid with Patrik Schumacher.
Project leader: Filippo Innocenti.
Project team: Fernando Perez Vera, Maurizio Meossi, Lorenzo Grifantini, Cedric Libert, Barbara Pfenningstorff, Matthias Frei, Brent Crittenden, Achim Gergen, Tamar Jacobs, Cornelius Schotthauer, Anneka Wegener, Thomas Vietzke.
Structural engineer: Adams Kara Taylor, Hanif Kara.
Service engineer: Hoare Lea, Phil Dow, Andrew Bullmore, Miller Hannah.
Lighting consultant: Hoare Lea, Dominic Meyrick.
Consultants: Abt srl, David Sabatello, Ares srl, Roberto Righini, Immo Consultant, Alessandra Albani.

NEW FAST TRAIN STATION, NAPLES

Client: TAV.
Design: Zaha Hadid & Patrik Schumacher.
Project architect / managing: Filippo Innocenti, Paola Cattarin.
Design team: Fernando Perez Vera, Ergian Alberg, Hon Kong Chee, Cesare Griffa, Karim Muallem, Steven Hatzellis.
Competition team: Thomas Vietzke, Jens Borstelmann, Robert Neumayr, Elena Perez, Adriano De Gioannis, Simon Kim, Selim Mimita.
Structural engineering: AKT– Hanif Kara.
Environmental engineering: MAX FORDHAM – Henry Luker.
Landscape design: GROSS MAX – Eelco Hooftman.
Local team: INTERPLAN 2 SRL – Alessandro Gubitosi.

TEMPORARY GUGGENHEIM MUSEUM, TOKYO

Client: Guggenheim Museum, NY.
Design: Zaha Hadid with Patrik Schumacher.
Design team: Gianluca Racana, Kenneth Bostock, Vivek V. Shankar.
Structural engineering: AKT– Hanif Kara.
Service engineer: Hoare Lea.
Lighting consultant: Hoare Lea.
Materials engineer: Tom Barker.

GUGGENHEIM MUSEUM, TAICHUNG

Client: Guggenheim Museum, NY.
Design: Zaha Hadid with Patrik Schumacher.

Project architect: Dillon Lin.
Design team: Jens Borstelmann, Thomas Vietzke, Yosuke Hayano.
Production team: Adriano De Gioannis, Selim Mimita, Juan-Ignacio Aranguren, Ken Bostock, Elena Perez, Ergian Alberg, Rocio Paz, Markus Planteu.
Structural engineer: Adams-Kara-Taylor, Hanif Kara, Andrew Murray, Sebastian Khourain, Reuben Brambleby, Stefano Strazzullo.
Services consultant: IDOM, Bilbao.
Cost consultant: IDOM UK, IDOM Bilbao.

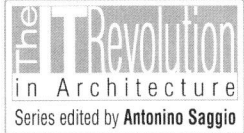

The Information Technology Revolution in Architecture is a new series reflecting on the effects the virtual dimension is having on architects and architecture in general. Each volume will examine a single topic, highlighting the essential aspects and exploring their relevance for the architects of today.

Series edited by **Antonino Saggio**

Other titles in this series:

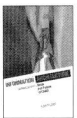

Information Architecture
Basis and Future of CAAD
Gerhard Schmitt
ISBN 3-7643-6092-5

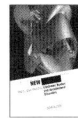

New Wombs
Electronic Bodies and Architectural Disorders
Maria Luisa Palumbo
ISBN 3-7643-6294-4

HyperArchitecture
Spaces in the Electronic Age
Luigi Prestinenza Puglisi
ISBN 3-7643-6093-3

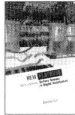

New Flatness
Surface Tension in Digital Architecture
Alicia Imperiale
ISBN 3-7643-6295-2

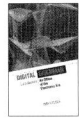

Digital Eisenman
An Office of the Electronic Era
Luca Galofaro
ISBN 3-7643-6094-1

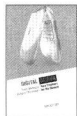

Digital Design
New Frontiers for the Objects
Paolo Martegani /
Riccardo Montenegro
ISBN 3-7643-6296-0

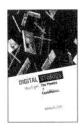

Digital Stories
The Poetics of Communication
Maia Engeli
ISBN 3-7643-6175-1

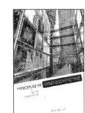

The Architecture of Intelligence
Derrick de Kerckhove
ISBN 3-7643-6451-3

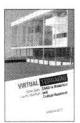

Virtual Terragni
CAAD in Historical and Critical Research
Mirko Galli / Claudia Mühlhoff
ISBN 3-7643-6174-3

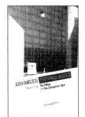

Advanced Technologies
Building in the Computer Age
Valerio Travi
ISBN 3-7643-6450-5

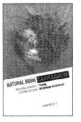

Natural Born CAADesigners
Young American Architects
Christian Pongratz /
Maria Rita Perbellini
ISBN 3-7643-6246-4

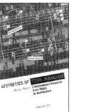

Aesthetics of Total Serialism
Contemporary Research from Music to Architecture
Markus Bandur
ISBN 3-7643-6449-1

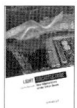

Light Architecture
New Edge City
Gianni Ranaulo
ISBN 3-7643-6564-1

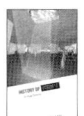

History of Form*Z
Pierluigi Serraino
ISBN 3-7643-6563-3

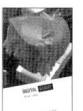

Digital Gehry
Material Resistance /
Digital Construction
Bruce Lindsey
ISBN 3-7643-6562-5

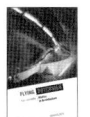

Flying Dutchmen
Motion in Architecture
Kari Jormakka
ISBN 3-7643-6639-7

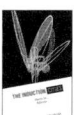

Induction Design
A Method for Evolutionary Design
Makoto Sei Watanabe
ISBN 3-7643-6641-9

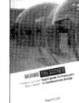

Behind the Scenes
Avant-garde Technologies
in Contemporary Design
Francesco De Luca / Marco Nardini
ISBN 3-7643-6737-7

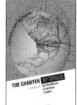

The Charter of Zurich
De Kerckhove Eisenman Saggio
Furio Barzon
ISBN 3-7643-6735-0

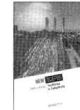

New Scapes
Territories of Complexity
Paola Gregory
ISBN 3-7643-6736-9

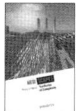

Hyperbodies
Toward an E-motive Architecture
Kaas Oosterhuis
ISBN 3-7643-6969-8

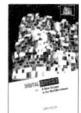

Digital Odyssey
A New Voyage in the Mediterranean
Ian+
ISBN 3-7643-6970-1

Mathland
From Flatland to Hypersurfaces
Michele Emmer
ISBN 3-7643-0149-X

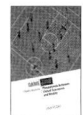

Game Zone
Playgrounds between
Virtual Scenarios and Reality
Alberto Iacovoni
ISBN 3-7643-0151-1